So you Flunked the Series 7 exam?

MARK PIANTANIDA

Copyright © 2013 Mark Piantanida

All rights reserved.

ISBN-13: 978-1489526199

THE AUDIO FILE TO ACCOMPANY THIS BOOK IS AVAILABLE AT FACEBOOK.COM/SOYOUFLUNKEDTHESERIES7EXAM

DEDICATION

To my father, the hardest working man I have ever known.

CONTENTS

1	Introduction	Pg 1
2	Why Does the Exam Seem So Hard?	Pg 2
3	Types of Options Questions	Pg 3
4	The Max Chart	Pg 4
5	Building Success	Pg 6
6	Adding Hints to the Chart	Pg 18
7	Recognizing the Strategies	Pg 22
8	The Mini Charts	Pg 48
9	Stock Split Effects on Options Positions	Pg 49
10	Applying Your Skills	Pg 51

INTRODUCTION

Walking into the office after passing the Series 7 exam is a great experience. Your manager and co-workers congratulate you, smile, and shake your hand. You know with certainty that dinner tonight will be a celebration. It's a very nice experience. I believe that you will experience this soon.

There are thousands of books written to educate people on the topic of investing. This book is not one of them. This book will not assist your understanding of the financial markets or financial products. The aim of this book is very simple. The aim of this book is for you to pass the test.

Financial Services companies provide test candidates with a very comprehensive book and practice tests. This is enough for some students, but not all of them. If you're reading this now, you may have already had an unsuccessful attempt at the exam. The good news is that your confidence is about to soar.

-It is impossible to overstate my next comment-

The Series 7 exam is a relatively easy test with the exception of one section – stock options. **Stock option exam questions keep most would-be stockbrokers from ever passing the exam.**

You must understand that this book and audio file are designed to be used as a supplement to your regular study material. Your regular study material will show you a detailed overview of what is covered on the exam, and will provide you with practice questions designed to prepare you for the exam. This book is not a generalized study manual covering a broad overview of what is on the exam-there are plenty of study guides already on the market for this purpose. This manual will focus solely on the section which, in my humble opinion, has been the single greatest reason for failure of the Series 7 exam.

This book and audio file will equip you with a way to come up with the answers to some of the hardest test questions very quickly. No wasted time. No over-thinking questions. Get a correct answer, and move on.

This book will teach you how to draw a chart that will provide you with instant answers to many options questions presented to you on the test. The chart is designed to answer the questions regarding the maximum gain, breakeven, and maximum loss on different strategies. However, in doing so you will also begin to recognize the different strategies as you memorize the chart layout.

When you go in to take the exam (even before touching the computer) you'll draw the chart on the paper that the testing center provides. Personnel at the testing centers refer to this as a "brain dump." At this point, whenever certain options questions appear, you'll have the answer at-a-glance and you're getting yet another easy point. The author of this book used this technique and scored 95%.

To reiterate, this book and audio file are to be used as a supplemental study guide to be accompanied by the study material with which your firm has supplied you. It is designed to transform some of the hardest questions on the test into the easiest questions on the test.

WHY DOES THE EXAM SEEM SO HARD?

The Series 7 exam contains 250 questions.

The questions regarding stocks, bonds, mutual funds, and other common-sense investments usually pose no real threat to the test taker. However, stock options are **very** heavily weighted on the exam and appear challenging for most candidates:

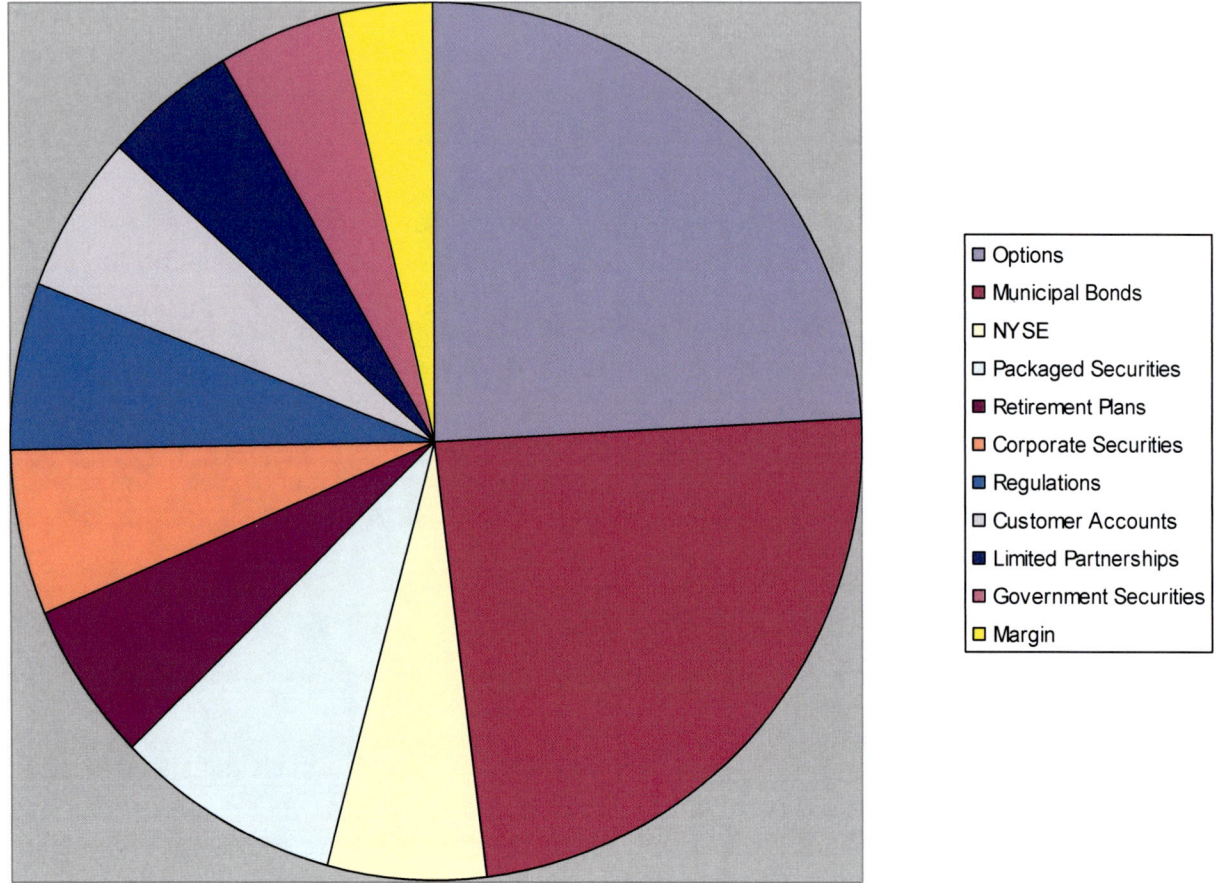

For many, the ability to answer stock options questions is the difference between failing the exam and successfully becoming licensed.

Options questions are actually two questions in one: Even before you can figure out the answer to the question, you have to understand *what position the investor even has in the first place-*

Is the investor buying a straight option?

Is this an uncovered call?

Is this a covered put?

What exactly, is a covered put?

Is the investor long with a put, or short with a call?

Is it a spread?

Is it a bullish spread?

Is it a bearish spread?

Is it a debit spread?

Should the options expire?

Is it a straddle?

Is it a long straddle or a short straddle?

It can make your head spin...

You may be asking yourself "Why are options questions so hard"? The answer is partially because:

An investor can buy or sell a stock option alone.

Or...an investor can combine the purchase or sale of an option with a stock position.

Or...an investor can combine the purchase or sale of an option with another option.

My first suggestion to you is this: Read the material given to you by your firm. Study all of the non-option related material in the Series 7 manual, skipping the options sections. Then, gain an understanding of options basics. Read the first chapter on options to familiarize yourself with the basics of options. Calls and puts. Buying and selling calls and puts. Read the material on selling options, covered and uncovered. Read about what a spread is and read what a straddle is. Gain a basic understanding. Some exam questions have to be completely thought through. They will require a greater amount of focus and concentration. However, you will find with other questions that <u>if you can read a question and identify the position, many times you can pull the answer from your chart in a matter of seconds.</u>

THE MAX CHART

At this time, I would like to present the chart that we'll be building together so you'll know what you are aiming for. This is the finished product. It may take a few days to commit this to memory to the point where you can draw it without looking. This is time well spent as it will transform some of the hardest questions on the exam into the easiest ones. In the next section, we will begin building the chart step-by-step.

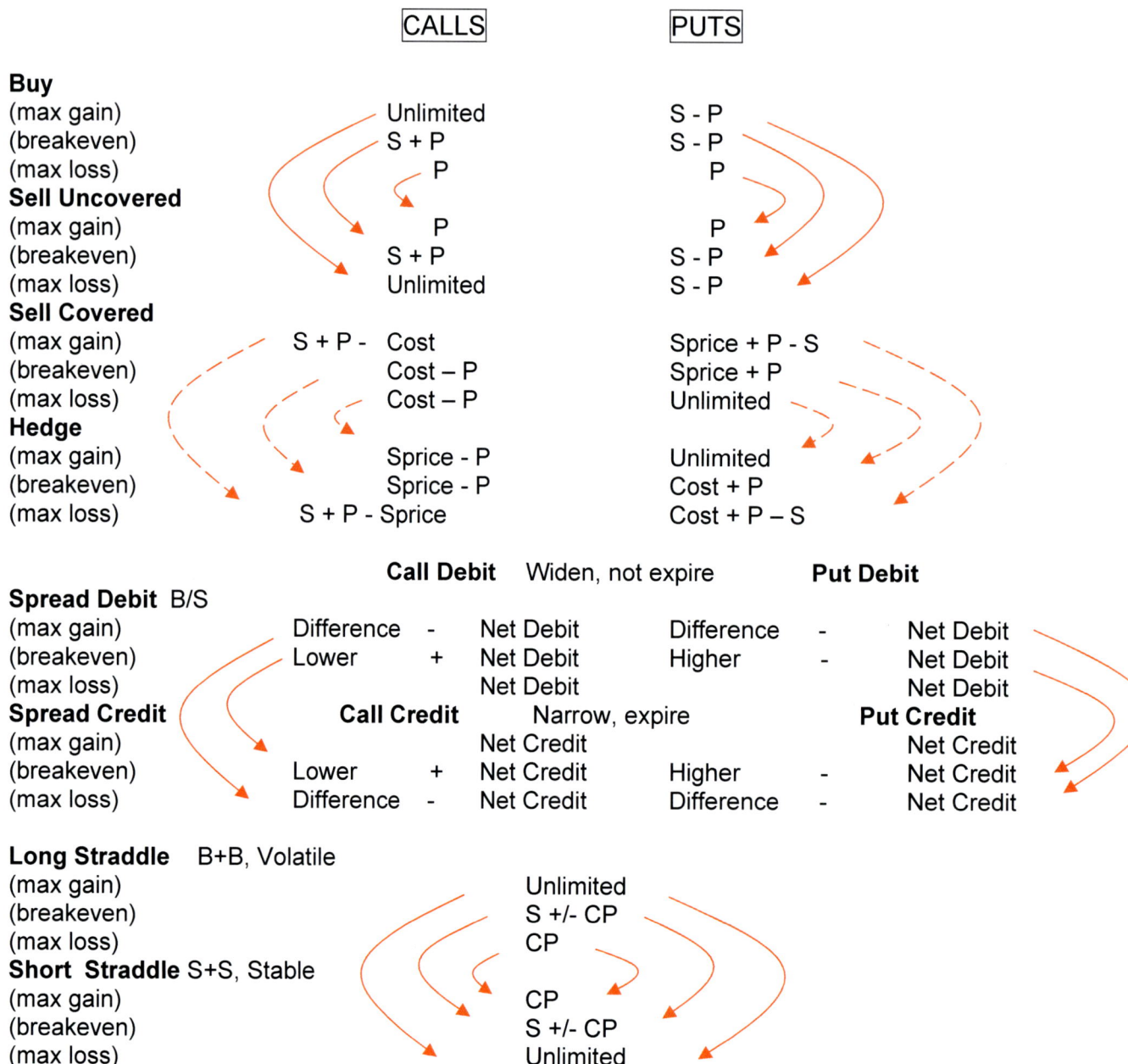

This is the short-hand version that I drew when sitting for the exam, which worked extremely well:

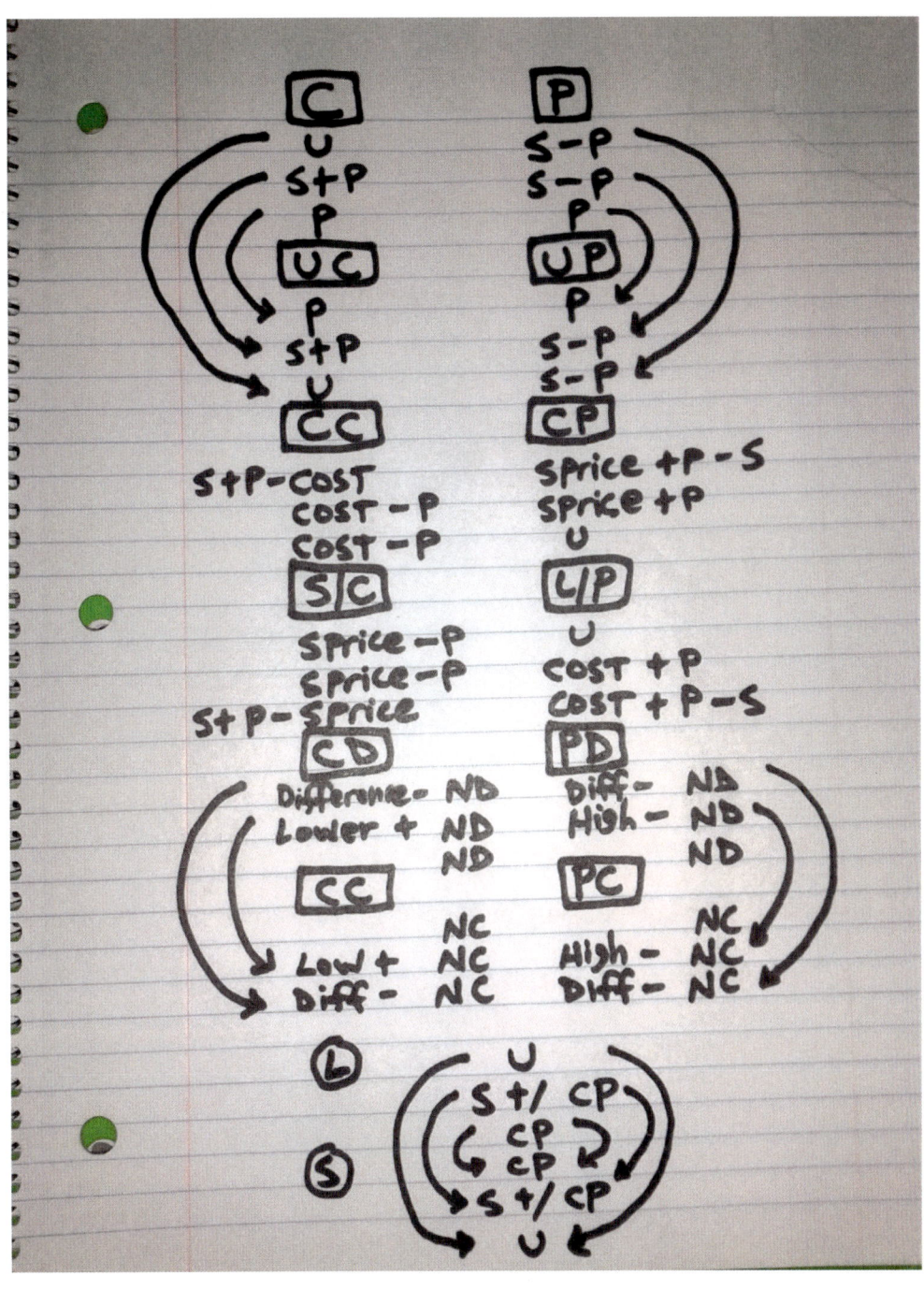

THE AUDIO FILE TO ACCOMPANY THIS BOOK IS AVAILABLE AT FACEBOOK.COM/SOYOUFLUNKEDTHESERIES7EXAM

BUILDING SUCCESS

Let's start building our chart.

There are only **two types of stock options**-calls and puts.

To begin writing the chart, let's put "calls" on the left, and "puts" on the right:

| CALLS | PUTS |

There are only **seven strategies** applied to stock options on the exam:

Buy

Sell uncovered

Sell covered

Hedge

Spread debit

Spread credit

Straddle

By listing the strategies down the left hand side of the chart, our beginning outline will look like this:

| CALLS | PUTS |

Buy
Sell Uncovered
Sell Covered
Hedge
Spread Debit
Spread Credit
Straddle

Next, place "maximum gain", "breakeven", and "maximum loss" under the seven strategies. The chart outline will now appear like this:

|CALLS| |PUTS|

Buy
(max gain)
(breakeven)
(max loss)
Sell Uncovered
(max gain)
(breakeven)
(max loss)
Sell Covered
(max gain)
(breakeven)
(max loss)
Hedge
(max gain)
(breakeven)
(max loss)
Spread Debit
(max gain)
(breakeven)
(max loss)
Spread Credit
(max gain)
(breakeven)
(max loss)
Straddle
(max gain)
(breakeven)
(max loss)

Now, let's stop here for a minute…Remember-even before you can figure out the answer to the question, you have to understand *what position the investor even has in the first place.* We're going to read a question, pull out key pieces of information (strike price, premium, cost of stock, short sale price, etc) and plug their abbreviations into the chart to create formulas that we can use to arrive at the correct answer. (strike price = S, premium = P, etc). We will break the 7 strategies into 7 sections and complete them one at a time. **After each new section is added, please take out a blank white piece of paper and start building the chart to that point.** Repetition is key.

THE AUDIO FILE TO ACCOMPANY THIS BOOK IS AVAILABLE AT FACEBOOK.COM/SOYOUFLUNKEDTHESERIES7EXAM

Section One – Buying Calls and Puts

The uppermost part of the chart illustrates simply buying a call (on the left) or buying a put (on the right). An example of a question would be, "An investor buys an ABC Feb 100 **call** for a premium of $4". With this information, we know that the investor has purchased a call with a strike price of 100 and has paid a premium of $4. Therefore, looking at the chart his maximum gain is unlimited, his breakeven is the strike price + the premium (100 + 4 = 104), and his maximum loss is the premium that he paid ($4).

	CALLS	PUTS
Buy		
(max gain)	Unlimited	
(breakeven)	S + P	
(max loss)	P	

But what if the question posed was "An investor buys an ABC Feb 100 **put** for a premium of $4"? With this information, we know that the investor has bought a put with a strike price of 100 and has paid a premium of $4. Therefore, looking at the chart his maximum gain is the strike price – the premium (100 - 4 = 96), his breakeven is also the strike price - the premium (100 - 4 = 96), and his maximum loss is the premium that he paid ($4):

	CALLS	PUTS
Buy		
(max gain)	Unlimited	S - P
(breakeven)	S + P	S - P
(max loss)	P	P

You now have one of the seven blocks completed: Buying calls and puts. If a test question should appear asking "What is the breakeven point on a purchase of a call option with a strike price of 50 and a premium of $3?" you can look for the answer "$53".

In fact, you now have a possible six easy points on the Series 7 exam …

It is HIGHLY advisable to stop at this point and practice writing the chart above on a blank piece of paper. Write it out ten times. Commit it to memory.

Section Two – Selling Uncovered Calls and Puts.

It is very important to note that if you have a question that tells you that an investor has **sold** a call or a put and there is **no mention** of the investor being long or short the stock, it's an **uncovered** position. (This simply means that you look at section two of your chart.)

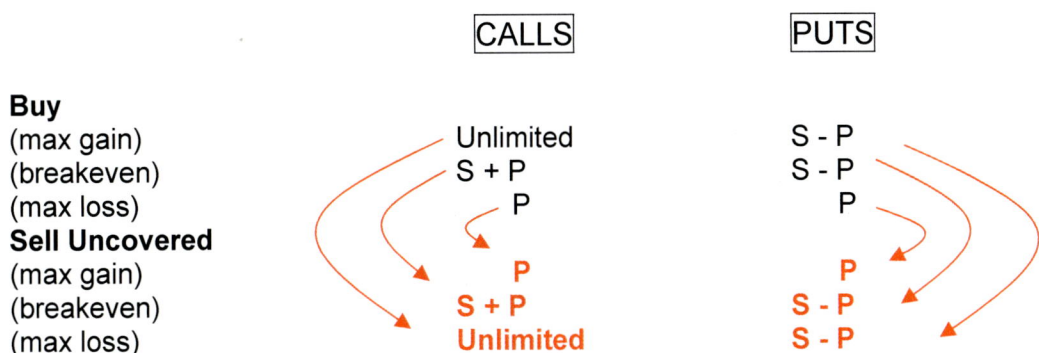

Do you notice the "mirror image" between the maximum gain, breakeven, and maximum loss between buying options and selling them uncovered?

Yes, for section two, you simply bring down the calculations in reverse order and you're done. Draw the arrows for extra guidance.

Memorizing only this far will arm you with the answers to 12 possible questions that you may encounter.

It is HIGHLY advisable to stop at this point and practice writing the chart above on a blank piece of paper. Write it out ten times. Commit it to memory.

Section Three – Selling Covered Calls and Puts

It is very important to note that if you have a question that tells you that an investor has **sold** a call or a put and there **is mention of the investor being long or short the stock, it's a covered position**. (This simply means that you look at section three of your chart.)

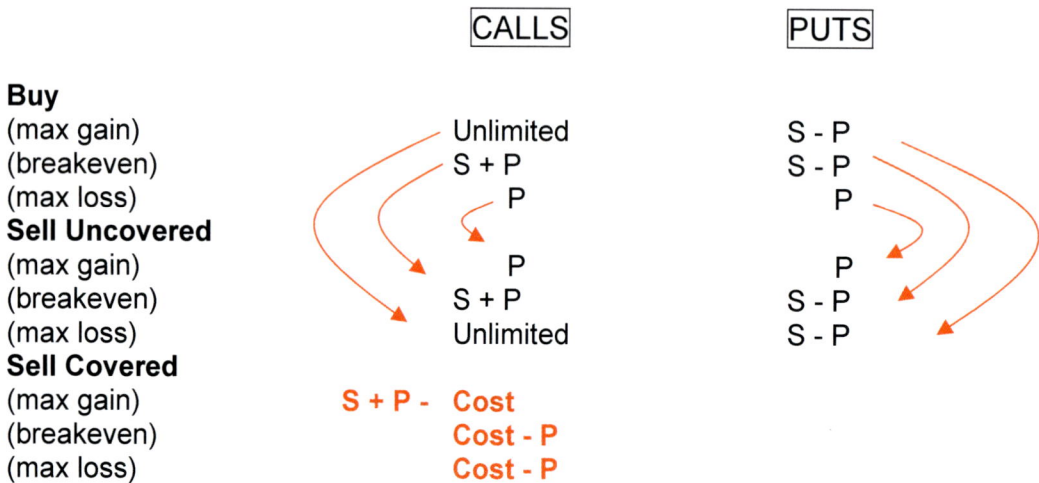

	CALLS	PUTS
Buy		
(max gain)	Unlimited	S - P
(breakeven)	S + P	S - P
(max loss)	P	P
Sell Uncovered		
(max gain)	P	P
(breakeven)	S + P	S - P
(max loss)	Unlimited	S - P
Sell Covered		
(max gain)	S + P - Cost	
(breakeven)	Cost - P	
(max loss)	Cost - P	

An example may be similar to this "An investor sells an ABC Feb 30 call at a premium of **$4 and he owns 100 shares of ABC stock at 26**. What is his breakeven point on the position"? This is an example of a covered call. The investor owns the stock, and he's selling options against it to generate income from the premium. Note that the investor **bought stock** and **sold** a call.

If you pull out the strike price, the premium and the cost of the stock, you can very quickly arrive at the answers to the maximum gain, breakeven and maximum loss figures. This is relatively easy to commit to memory as all three formulas have the word "cost" representing the cost of the stock. (Simply add "S+P - " on the upper formula and "– P" on the lower two).

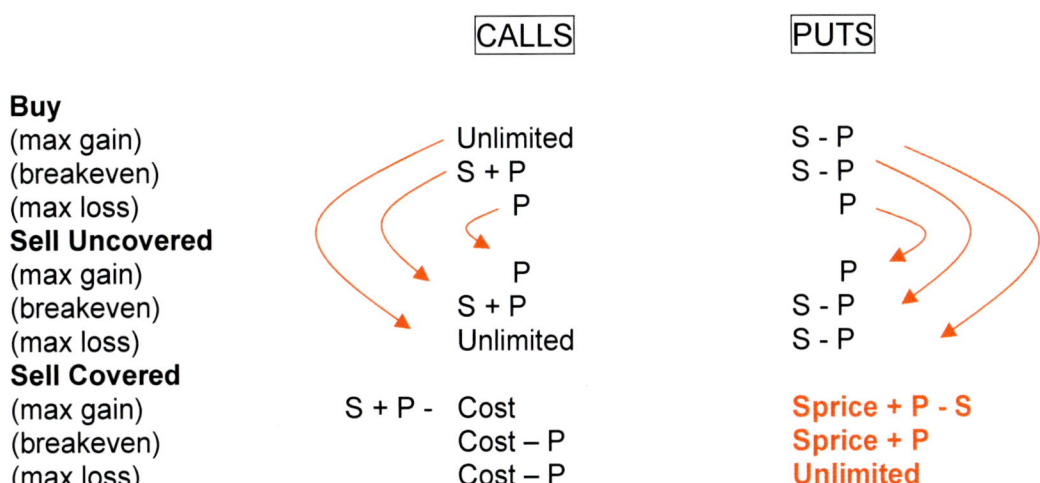

In the last example, the investor **bought stock** and **sold** a call. In covered put writing, the investor **sells stock short** and **sells a put short**. Don't get confused or frustrated here-let the chart simplify this for you. There are only three strategies above. We know that we're selling options, so the "buy" block is out. There is stock involved, so this can't be an "uncovered" position. The investor sold a put, so it can't be on the left "call" side of the chart…the only possibility is in red…elimination is the key here.

I'll give you an example to spot this:

"An investor sold short 100 shares of ABC at 36. He also sold one ABC put at 2. What's his breakeven?" Your thought process should be "Stock involved=covered. He sold a put, so it's on the put side of the chart. Therefore, in section three it says that the breakeven would be the short price (Sprice) + premium". Putting the numbers in the chart gives us 36 + 2 = 38. The formulas on this one should be an easy memorization for you as well.

It is HIGHLY advisable to stop at this point and practice writing the chart above on a blank piece of paper. Write it out ten times. Commit it to memory.

| **Section Four – Hedging** |

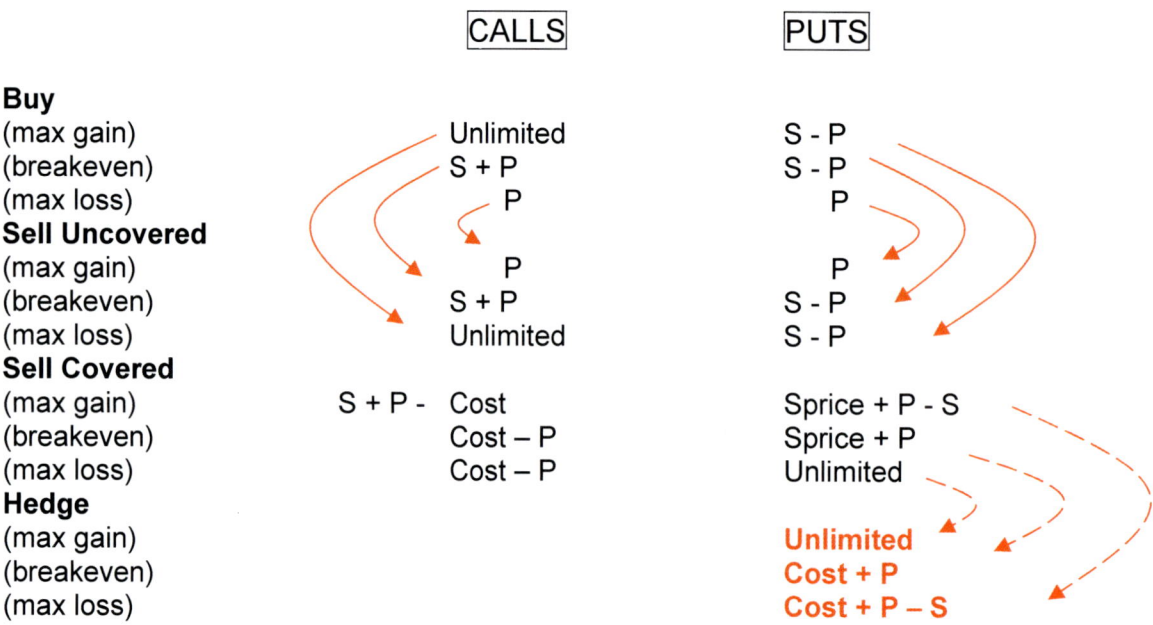

	CALLS	PUTS
Buy		
(max gain)	Unlimited	S - P
(breakeven)	S + P	S - P
(max loss)	P	P
Sell Uncovered		
(max gain)	P	P
(breakeven)	S + P	S - P
(max loss)	Unlimited	S - P
Sell Covered		
(max gain)	S + P - Cost	Sprice + P - S
(breakeven)	Cost – P	Sprice + P
(max loss)	Cost – P	Unlimited
Hedge		
(max gain)		**Unlimited**
(breakeven)		**Cost + P**
(max loss)		**Cost + P – S**

Hedging with options is an easy strategy to explain. I'll start with the "put" side. Imagine that you purchase a stock at $100 and the very next day it drops suddenly down to $50 per share. You would be down 50 dollars per share. However, If you bought a $100 put option at the time that you purchased the stock you would still be able to sell the stock at $100! They call this strategy "a cheap form of insurance". Note that you can exercise your put and sell the stock, or, as the stock drops you have a profit on the put side dollar-for-dollar to offset the stock loss. (You buy stock and buy a put for protection).

You may have noticed the dotted lines between sections 3 and 4 of the Max Chart. This is because there is not an *exact* mirror image. However, please note that **the Hedging strategy formulas are a mirror image of the Sell Covered strategies with the words "Sprice" and "Cost" interchanged** in the lower section. Therefore, when working on sections 3 and 4 you should memorize section 3, then use the mirror image for section 4 but substitute the word "Sprice" for "Cost" and "Cost" for "Sprice" once you get to the Hedging section.

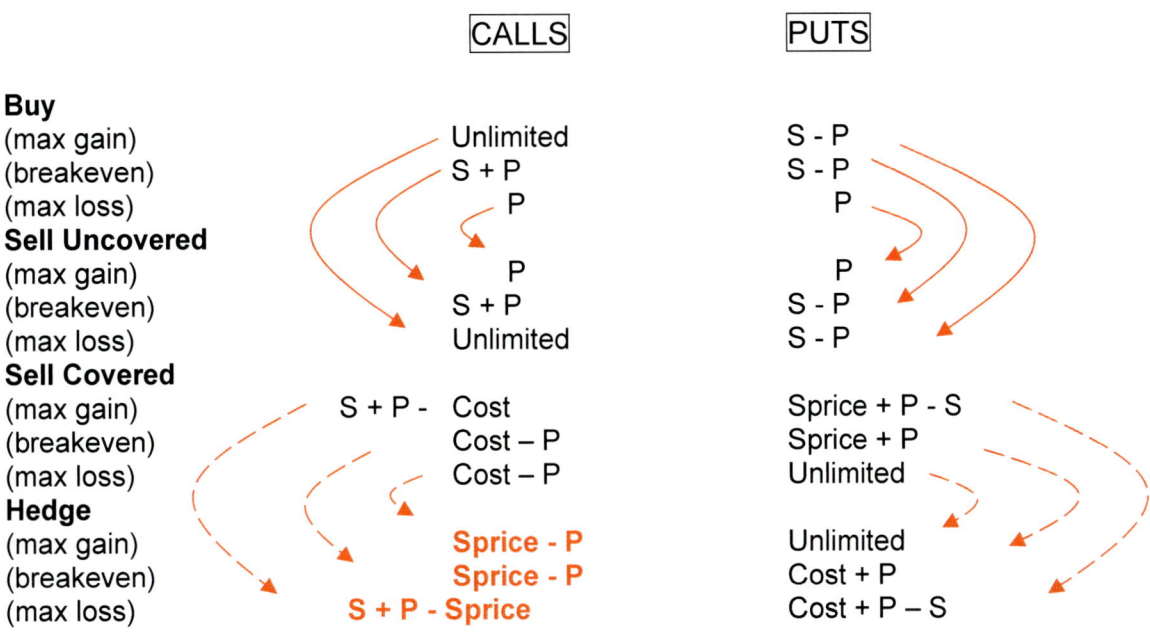

		CALLS	PUTS
Buy			
(max gain)		Unlimited	S - P
(breakeven)		S + P	S - P
(max loss)		P	P
Sell Uncovered			
(max gain)		P	P
(breakeven)		S + P	S - P
(max loss)		Unlimited	S - P
Sell Covered			
(max gain)		S + P - Cost	Sprice + P - S
(breakeven)		Cost – P	Sprice + P
(max loss)		Cost – P	Unlimited
Hedge			
(max gain)		Sprice - P	Unlimited
(breakeven)		Sprice - P	Cost + P
(max loss)		S + P - Sprice	Cost + P – S

Conversely, if you short a stock and you're concerned that its value could increase, a call option will give you the right to purchase the stock at the strike price prior to expiration. For example, if an investor were to short a stock at $50 per share and the stock rapidly increased to $100 per share, the investor could simply exercise his call option and purchase the stock at $50 to cover his short position. Again, a cheap form of insurance.

I would begin the memorization of this section by writing the word "Sprice" three times.

*Do not get the hedging strategies confused with covered selling simply because stock is mentioned. Hedging involves **buying** options. Covered selling is **selling** options.

It is HIGHLY advisable to stop at this point and practice writing the chart above on a blank piece of paper. Write it out ten times. Commit it to memory.

Sections Five and Six – Spreads

A spread is when an investor buys a call and sells a call, or he buys a put and sells a put (a buy/sell combination). If this is the case, look immediately to sections five and six on the chart. The net debit or credit will be the difference in the premiums.

There are four different types of spreads. Call debit, put debit, call credit, and put credit. Due to this, I'll be noting the different columns with headings. Simply continue to put the calls on the left, and the puts on the right. The debits are in the top debit area, and the credits are in the credit area on the bottom.

Luckily, we're coming to another "mirror image" in the spread section. I'm showing them all together and I'll build the formulas within the section.

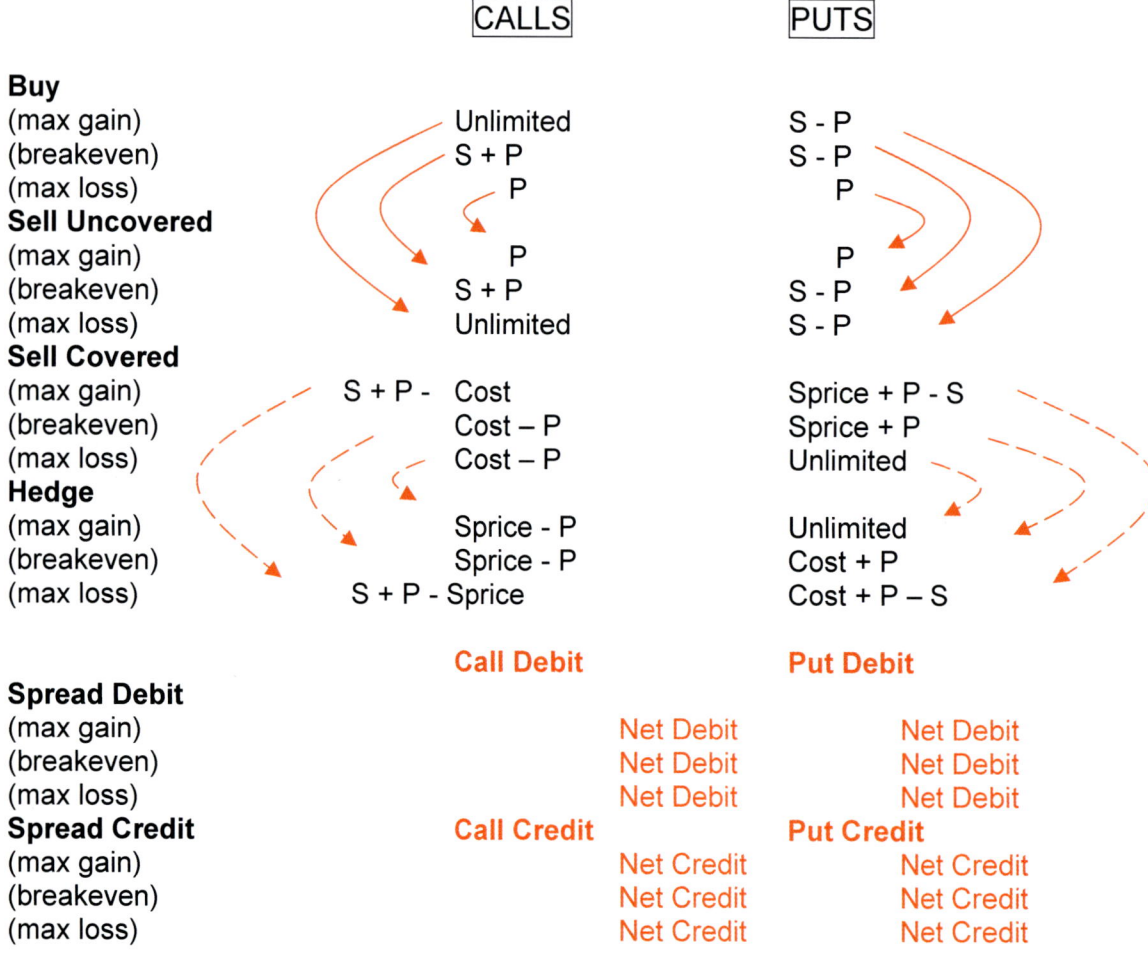

	CALLS	PUTS
Buy		
(max gain)	Unlimited	S - P
(breakeven)	S + P	S - P
(max loss)	P	P
Sell Uncovered		
(max gain)	P	P
(breakeven)	S + P	S - P
(max loss)	Unlimited	S - P
Sell Covered		
(max gain)	S + P - Cost	Sprice + P - S
(breakeven)	Cost – P	Sprice + P
(max loss)	Cost – P	Unlimited
Hedge		
(max gain)	Sprice - P	Unlimited
(breakeven)	Sprice - P	Cost + P
(max loss)	S + P - Sprice	Cost + P – S
	Call Debit	**Put Debit**
Spread Debit		
(max gain)	Net Debit	Net Debit
(breakeven)	Net Debit	Net Debit
(max loss)	Net Debit	Net Debit
Spread Credit	**Call Credit**	**Put Credit**
(max gain)	Net Credit	Net Credit
(breakeven)	Net Credit	Net Credit
(max loss)	Net Credit	Net Credit

THE AUDIO FILE TO ACCOMPANY THIS BOOK IS AVAILABLE AT FACEBOOK.COM/SOYOUFLUNKEDTHESERIES7EXAM

To build the spread section of the chart, first place the "call" and "put" headings into the chart ("calls" on left and "puts" on the right in keeping with the format). "Debits" on the top, and "credits" on the bottom (in keeping with the format on the left side). Then simply place six Net Debit on the top, six Net Credit on the bottom.

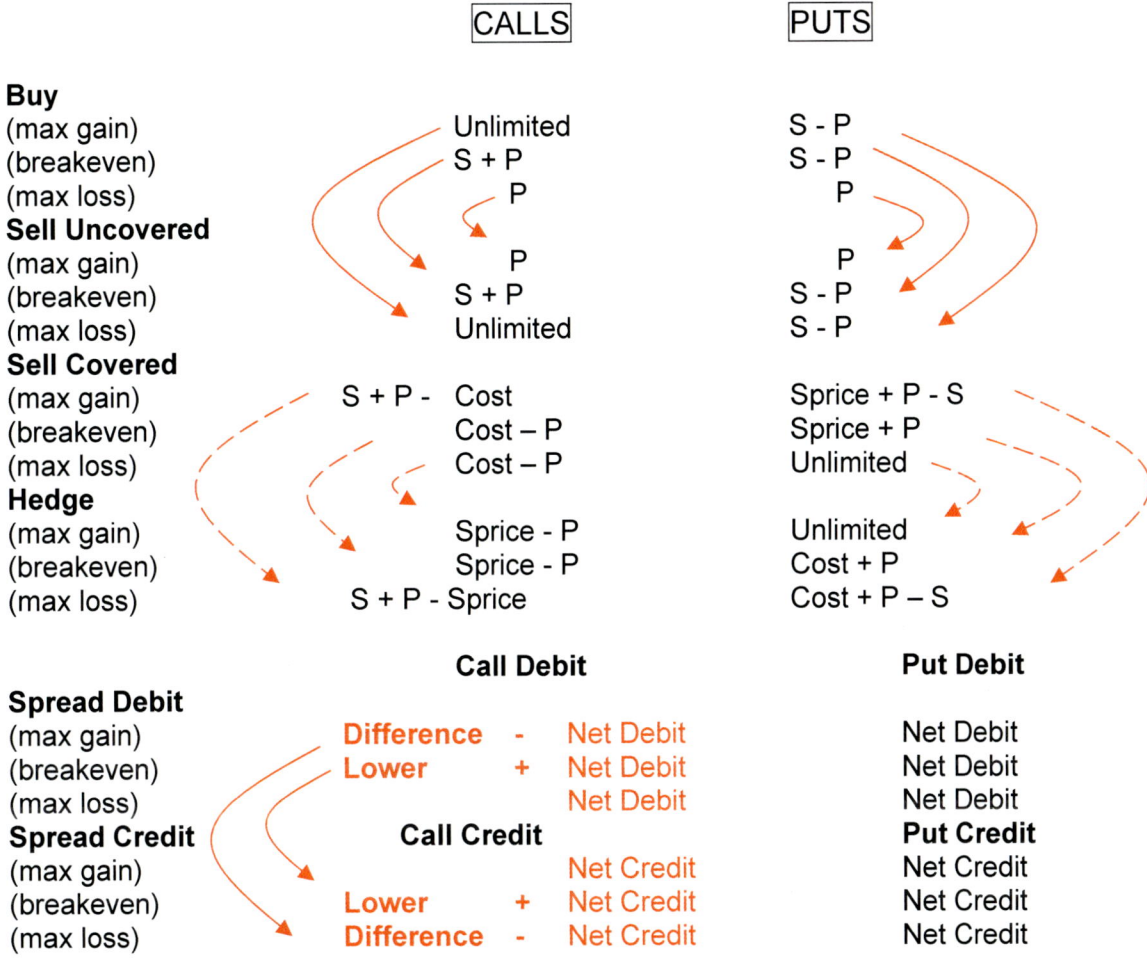

As you'll recall from the study material provided from your sponsor, when working with spreads, you'll be figuring out the differences in the strike prices as well as the net debit or credit. This difference in strike prices is represented in the chart as the word "difference". The words "lower" and "higher" are used to represent the lower or higher strike prices of the two contracts.

After the headings, Net Debits and Net Credits are outlined I simply write down the left side "Difference minus" and "Lower plus". Then, bring them down just as you did with the mirror image in the upper part of the chart.

THE AUDIO FILE TO ACCOMPANY THIS BOOK IS AVAILABLE AT FACEBOOK.COM/SOYOUFLUNKEDTHESERIES7EXAM

To complete the right side of the Spread section, simply write "Difference minus" and "Higher minus" and apply the mirror image:

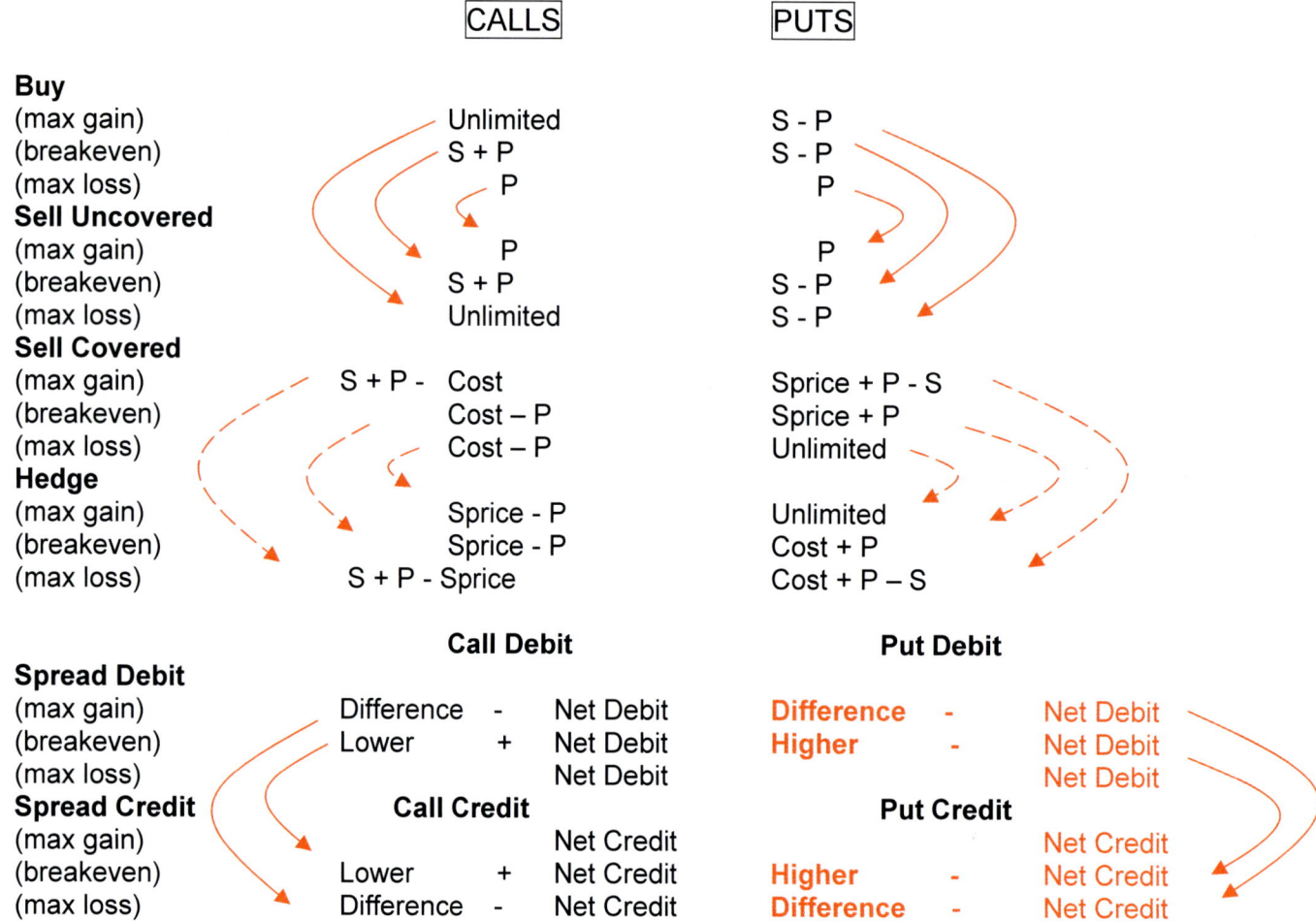

It is HIGHLY advisable to stop at this point and practice writing the chart above on a blank piece of paper. Write it out ten times. Commit it to memory.

Section Seven – Straddles

Straddles are the buying of both a call and put (long straddle) or the selling of both a call and put (short straddle). An easy way to remember this is that a long straddle is a "buy and a buy" and a short straddle is a "sell and a sell". The "CP" below stands for the combined premium. There are two breakeven points: the strike price + the combined premium and the strike price – the combined premium.

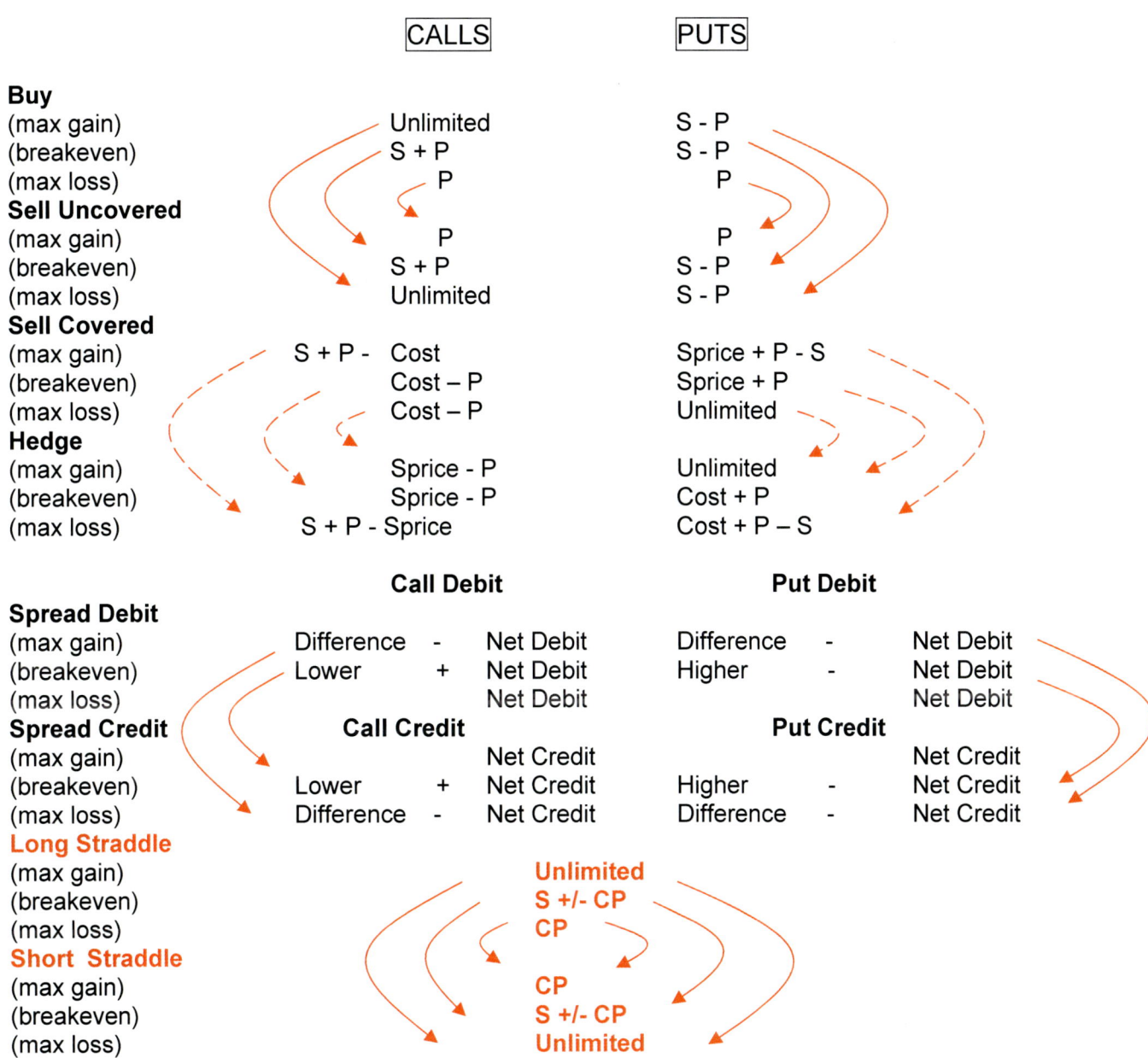

	CALLS	PUTS
Buy		
(max gain)	Unlimited	S - P
(breakeven)	S + P	S - P
(max loss)	P	P
Sell Uncovered		
(max gain)	P	P
(breakeven)	S + P	S - P
(max loss)	Unlimited	S - P
Sell Covered		
(max gain)	S + P - Cost	Sprice + P - S
(breakeven)	Cost – P	Sprice + P
(max loss)	Cost – P	Unlimited
Hedge		
(max gain)	Sprice - P	Unlimited
(breakeven)	Sprice - P	Cost + P
(max loss)	S + P - Sprice	Cost + P – S
	Call Debit	**Put Debit**
Spread Debit		
(max gain)	Difference - Net Debit	Difference - Net Debit
(breakeven)	Lower + Net Debit	Higher - Net Debit
(max loss)	Net Debit	Net Debit
	Call Credit	**Put Credit**
Spread Credit		
(max gain)	Net Credit	Net Credit
(breakeven)	Lower + Net Credit	Higher - Net Credit
(max loss)	Difference - Net Credit	Difference - Net Credit
Long Straddle		
(max gain)	Unlimited	
(breakeven)	S +/- CP	
(max loss)	CP	
Short Straddle		
(max gain)	CP	
(breakeven)	S +/- CP	
(max loss)	Unlimited	

It is HIGHLY advisable to stop at this point and practice writing the chart above on a blank piece of paper. Write it out ten times. Commit it to memory.

Adding Hints to the Chart

When dealing with options and employing strategies such as spreads and straddles, the thought process required can become confusing. To help recognize the strategy being described, a few hints spread throughout the chart can give you a huge advantage.

Recognizing Spreads:

A spread is when you buy a call and sell a call or you buy a put and you sell a put. It's a **buy/sell** combination. (The call or put part is the same.) To help remember this, we can place small letters (B/S) in this section to refresh our memory of the strategy quickly. For example, if you read a question which describes an investor that bought and sold calls, you can find the hint "B/S" in the spread section:

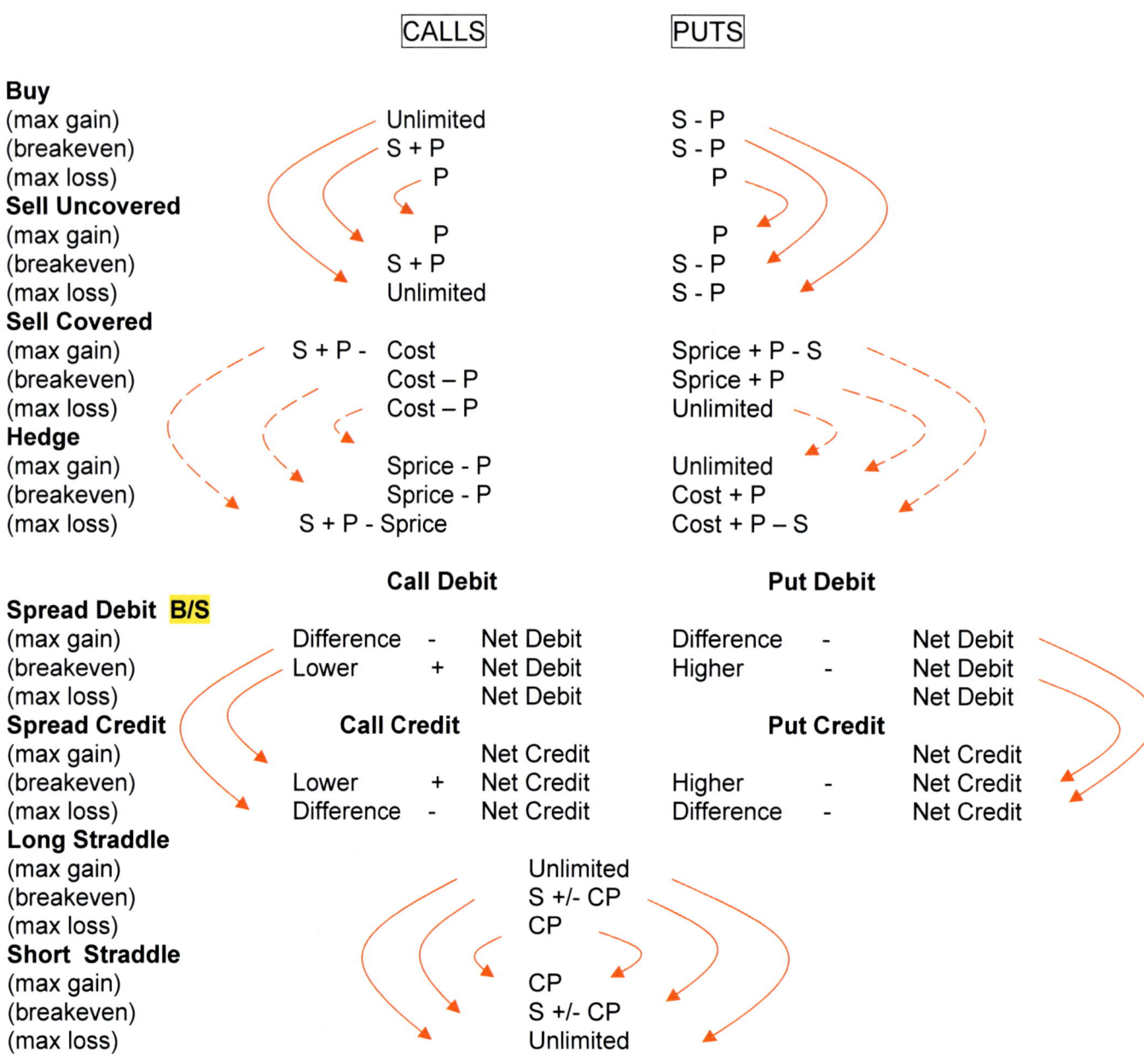

	CALLS	PUTS
Buy		
(max gain)	Unlimited	S - P
(breakeven)	S + P	S - P
(max loss)	P	P
Sell Uncovered		
(max gain)	P	P
(breakeven)	S + P	S - P
(max loss)	Unlimited	S - P
Sell Covered		
(max gain)	S + P - Cost	Sprice + P - S
(breakeven)	Cost – P	Sprice + P
(max loss)	Cost – P	Unlimited
Hedge		
(max gain)	Sprice - P	Unlimited
(breakeven)	Sprice - P	Cost + P
(max loss)	S + P - Sprice	Cost + P – S
	Call Debit	**Put Debit**
Spread Debit B/S		
(max gain)	Difference - Net Debit	Difference - Net Debit
(breakeven)	Lower + Net Debit	Higher - Net Debit
(max loss)	Net Debit	Net Debit
Spread Credit	**Call Credit**	**Put Credit**
(max gain)	Net Credit	Net Credit
(breakeven)	Lower + Net Credit	Higher - Net Credit
(max loss)	Difference - Net Credit	Difference - Net Credit
Long Straddle		
(max gain)	Unlimited	
(breakeven)	S +/- CP	
(max loss)	CP	
Short Straddle		
(max gain)	CP	
(breakeven)	S +/- CP	
(max loss)	Unlimited	

Narrow or Widen?

Due to the mechanics of spreads, an investor with a net credit spread will wish for both options to *expire worthless*. He will want the spread to *narrow*.

Conversely, an investor with a net debit spread will wish for his spread to widen, and will realize his maximum loss if both options expire worthless.

A simple note on the chart will keep you from having to spend time on this. There will be plenty of time after you have passed the test to read up on this subject. For now, simple hints on the chart will earn you the points and save you the time of thinking it through:

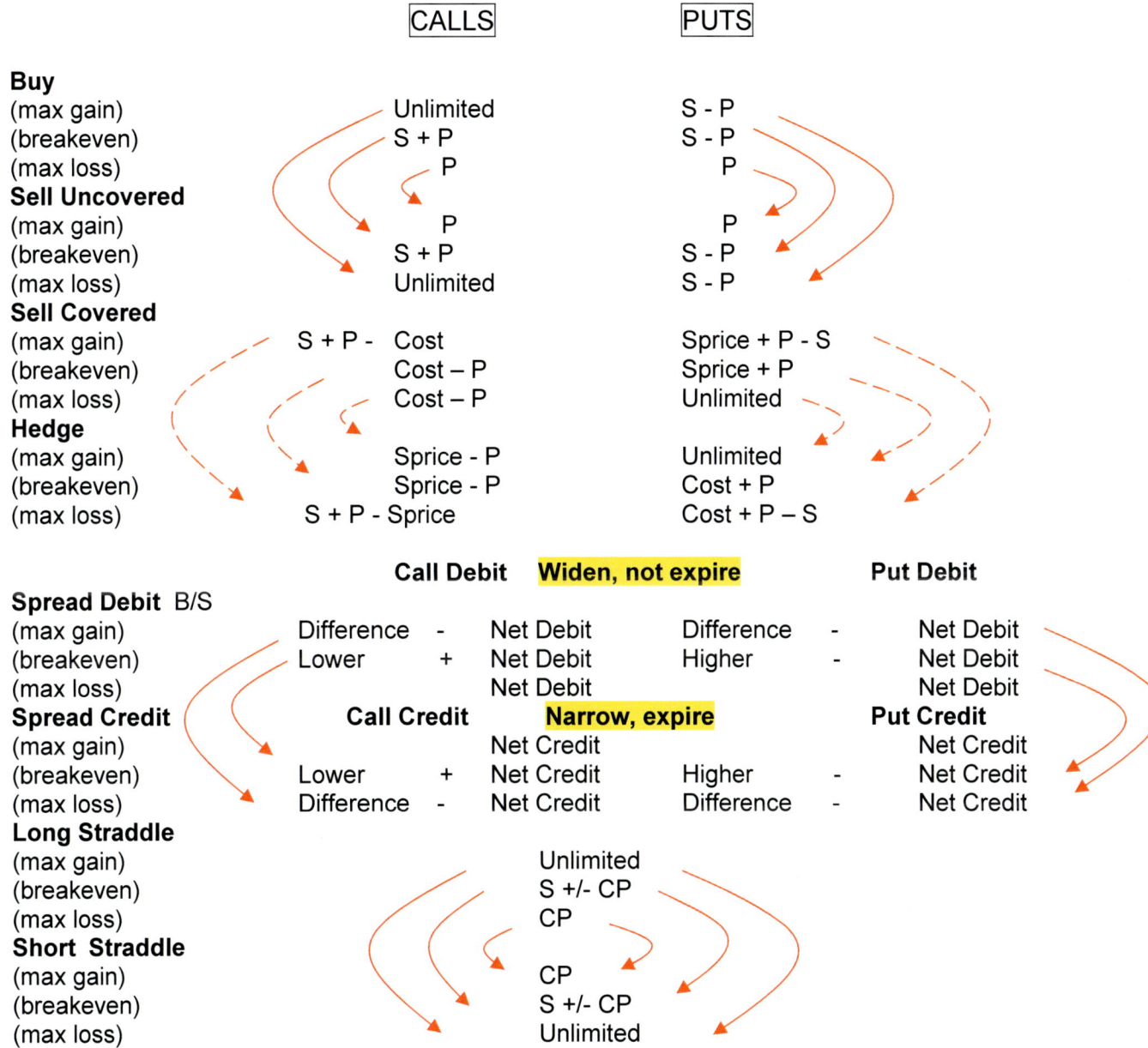

Recognizing straddles quickly:

A "straddle" is buying a call and a put or selling a call and a put simultaneously. It's a "**buy and a buy**", or a "**sell and a sell**". (The call and put part is different). To see this right away, we can place a "B+B" and "S+S" next to the words "Long Straddle" and "Short Straddle".

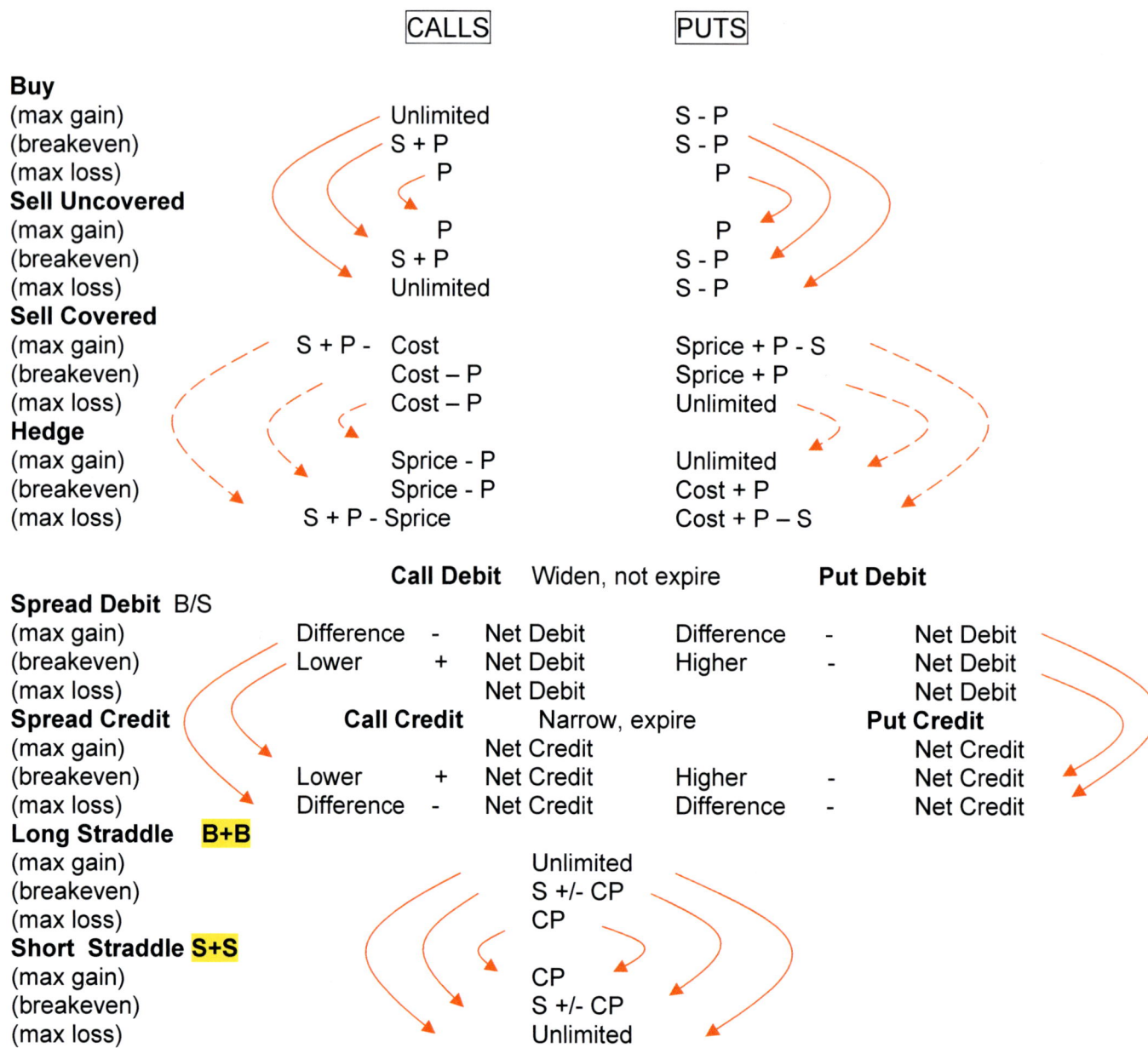

Volatility or Stability?

An investor who buys a straddle is anticipating a move in a stock, but is unsure of the direction that the stock will be moving. An investor that sells a straddle is not anticipating volatility, but stability. We can place a hint beside our last hints for straddles to quickly and easily answer this question:

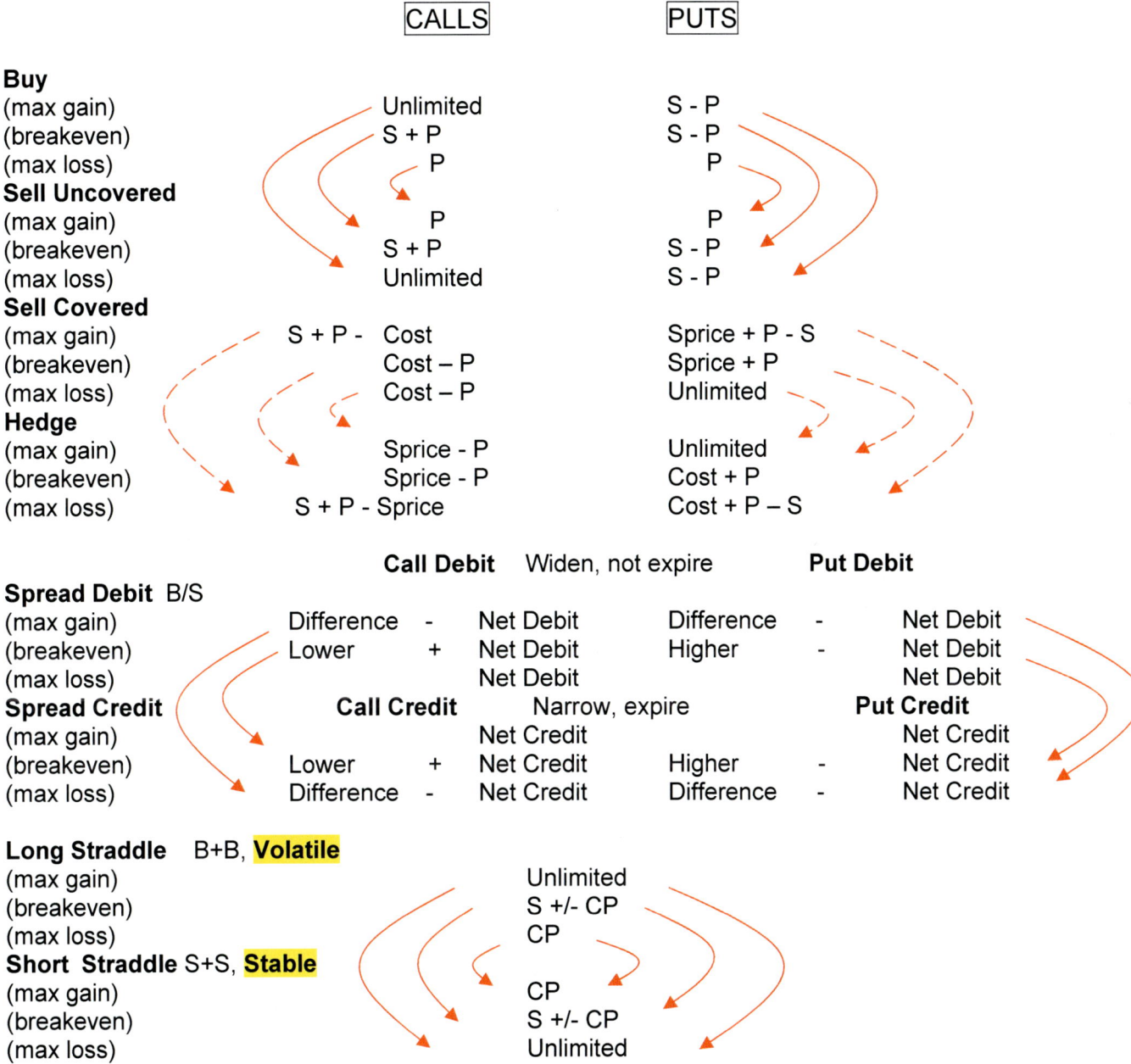

Armed with the ability to draw this chart at will, you'll be more prepared than you even realize. Please feel free to get creative. Add to it. Make it your own. If you would like to add formulas for stock splits, accrued interest on bonds, the taxable equivalent yield calculation, etc., please do so.

RECOGNIZING THE STRATEGIES

In the previous section, we constructed a chart that will give us the maximum gain, breakeven, and the maximum loss for the different strategies. In this section, I would like you to practice "seeing" the strategy that is being described in the question. I will give you simplified questions with a thought process enabling you to recognize the position, and apply it to the correct area of the chart. We'll work them out together. Then, we'll apply them to simulated exam questions.

	CALLS	PUTS
Buy		
(max gain)	Unlimited	S - P
(breakeven)	S + P	S - P
(max loss)	P	P
Sell Uncovered		
(max gain)	P	P
(breakeven)	S + P	S - P
(max loss)	Unlimited	S - P
Sell Covered		
(max gain)	S + P - Cost	Sprice + P - S
(breakeven)	Cost – P	Sprice + P
(max loss)	Cost – P	Unlimited
Hedge		
(max gain)	Sprice - P	Unlimited
(breakeven)	Sprice - P	Cost + P
(max loss)	S + P - Sprice	Cost + P – S

	CALLS		PUTS	
Spread Debit B/S	**Call Debit** Widen, not expire		**Put Debit**	
(max gain)	Difference	- Net Debit	Difference	- Net Debit
(breakeven)	Lower	+ Net Debit	Higher	- Net Debit
(max loss)		Net Debit		Net Debit
Spread Credit	**Call Credit** Narrow, expire		**Put Credit**	
(max gain)		Net Credit		Net Credit
(breakeven)	Lower	+ Net Credit	Higher	- Net Credit
(max loss)	Difference	- Net Credit	Difference	- Net Credit

Long Straddle B+B, Volatile	
(max gain)	Unlimited
(breakeven)	S +/- CP
(max loss)	CP
Short Straddle S+S, Stable	
(max gain)	CP
(breakeven)	S +/- CP
(max loss)	Unlimited

OPTION

Buy = Purchase of a call or put.

Sell Uncovered = Selling a call or put with NO MENTION of stock investment.

OPTION + STOCK (Buy option to hedge stock, sell to generate income on a covered position).

Sell Covered = Selling a call or put for income and the question mentions a stock position.

Hedge = Buying stock and buying a put for protection, or shorting stock and buying a call for protection.

OPTION + OPTION

Spread = A buy/sell combination on calls, or a buy/sell combination on puts.

Straddle = Buying a call and buying a put, or selling a call and selling a put.

The following simplified questions illustrate the thought process that should be used to identify the position which will be applied to the chart:

Question: An investor buys one ABC 35 put for a premium of $3. **Thought:** This is a buy of a put. Section 1 of the chart.

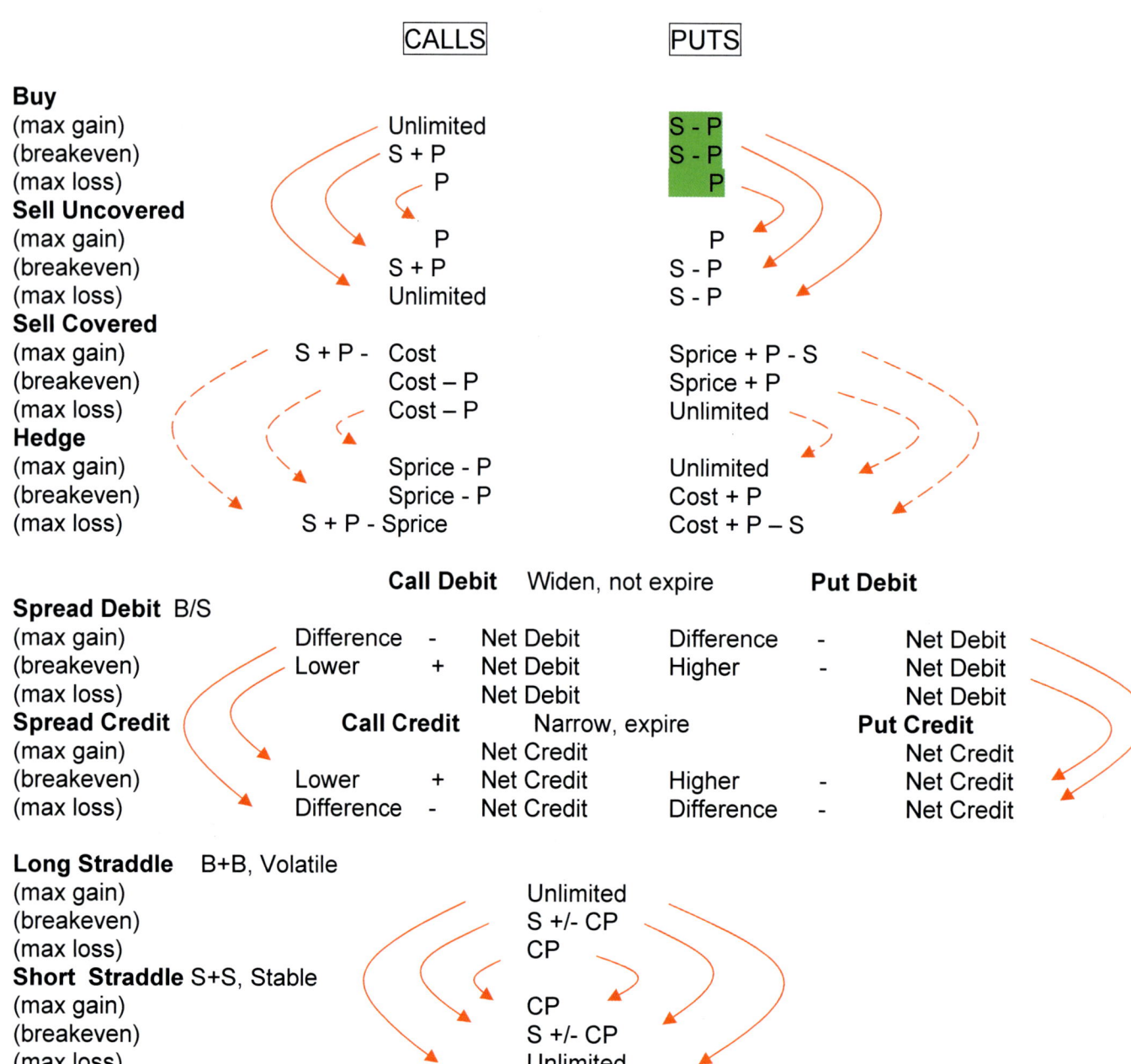

Question: An investor sells an ABC 25 call for a premium of $3. **Thought:** It's a sale of a call, and there is NO mention of stock owned. This is an uncovered call. Section 2 of the chart.

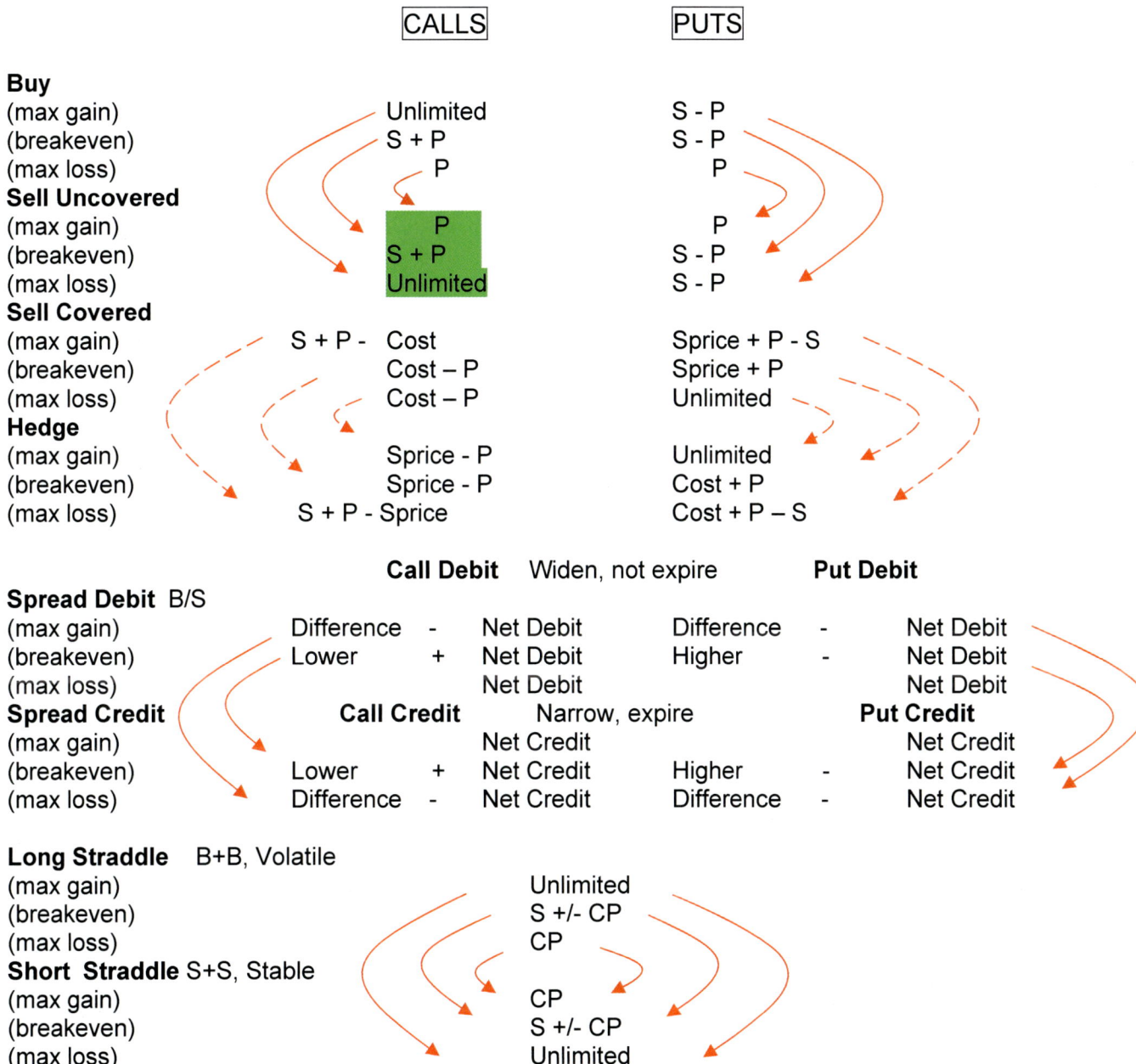

Question: An investor sells an ABC October 80 put for a premium of $4. **Thought:** It's a sale of a put, and there is NO mention of stock. This is an uncovered put. Section 2 of the chart.

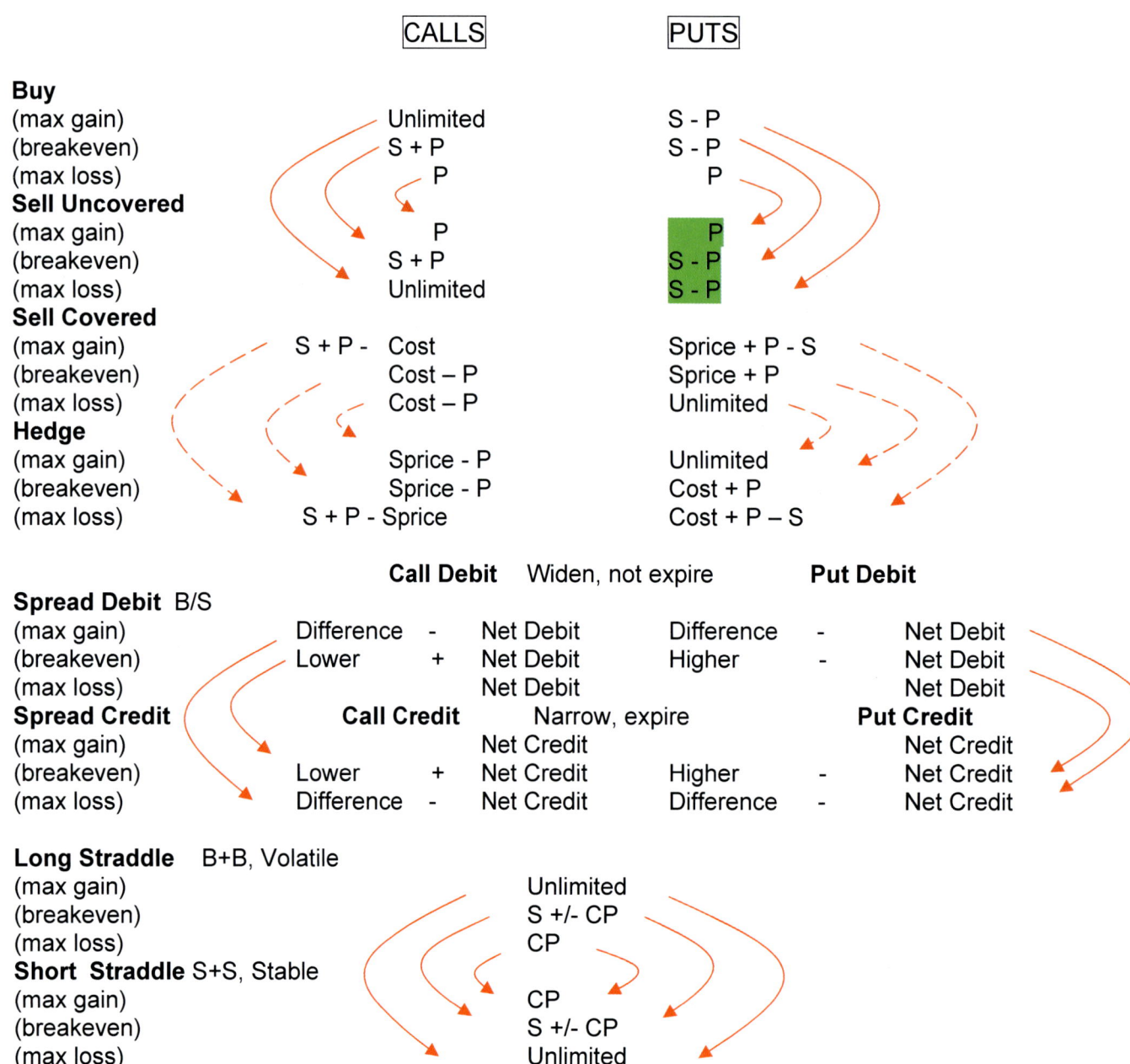

Question: An investor buys 100 shares of ABC at $32 and sells an ABC December 35 call for a premium of $4. **Thought:** It's a sale of a call, and there IS mention of stock. This is a covered call. Section 3 of the chart.

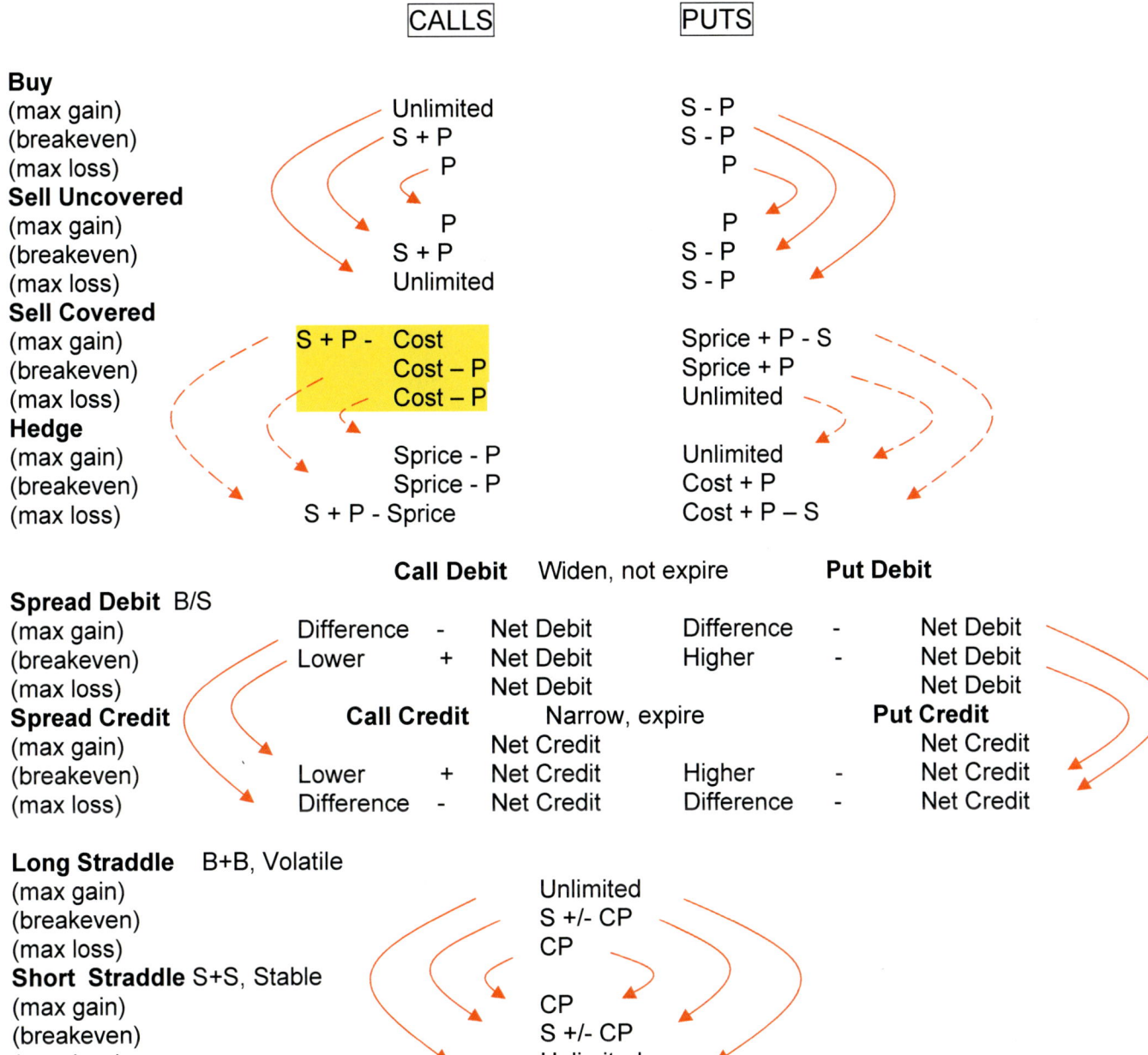

Question: An investor shorts 100 shares of ABC and sells an ABC put for a premium of $4. **Thought:** It's a sale of a put, and there IS mention of short stock. This is a covered put. Section 3 of the chart.

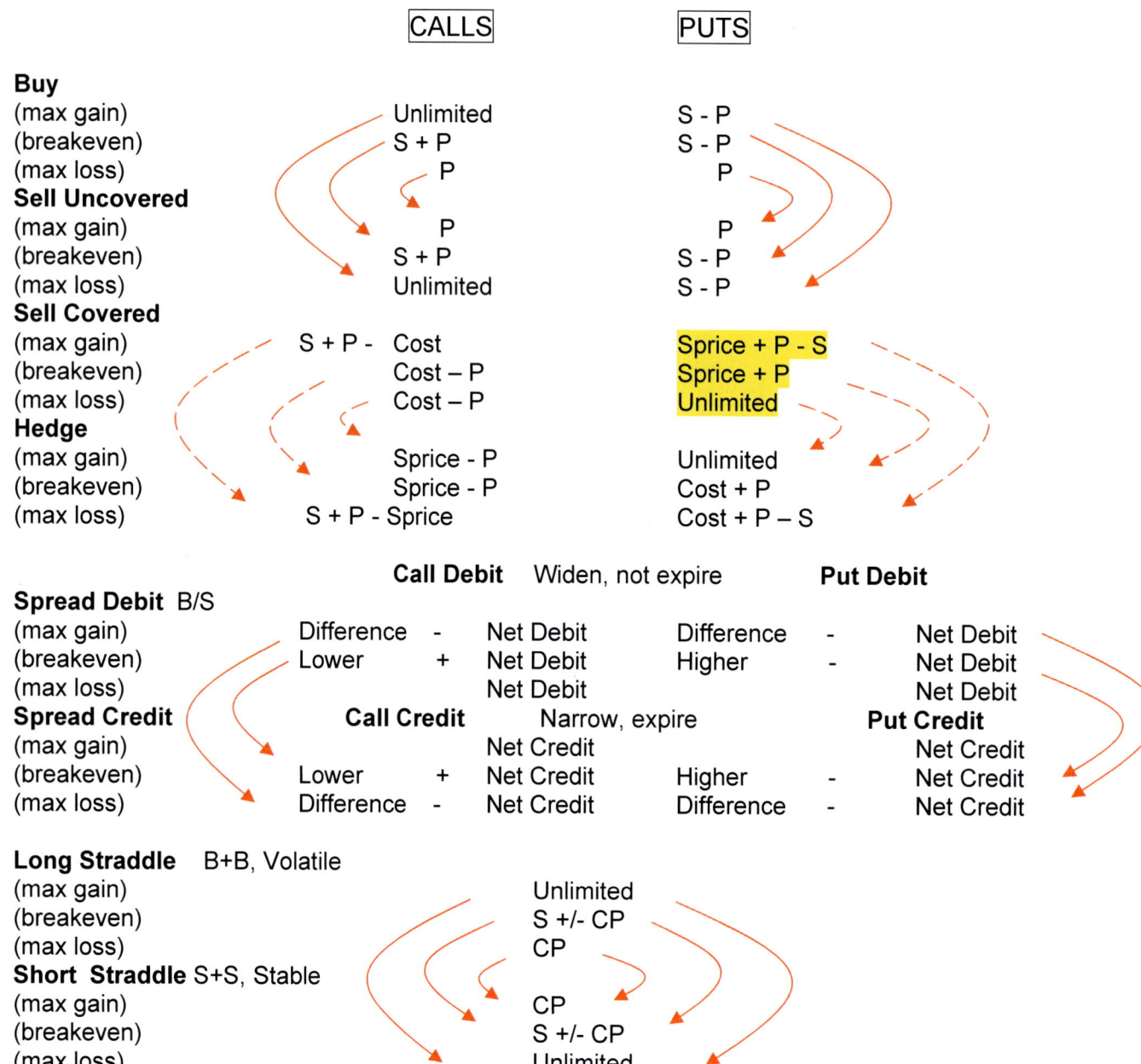

Question: An investor buys 100 shares of ABC and buys an ABC put for a premium of $4. **Thought**: It's a purchase of a put, and he owns the stock. The investor is hedging the stock with an options purchase. He's long with a put. Section 4 of the chart.

* Do not get the hedging strategies confused with covered selling simply because stock is mentioned. Hedging involves **buying** options. Covered selling is **selling** options.

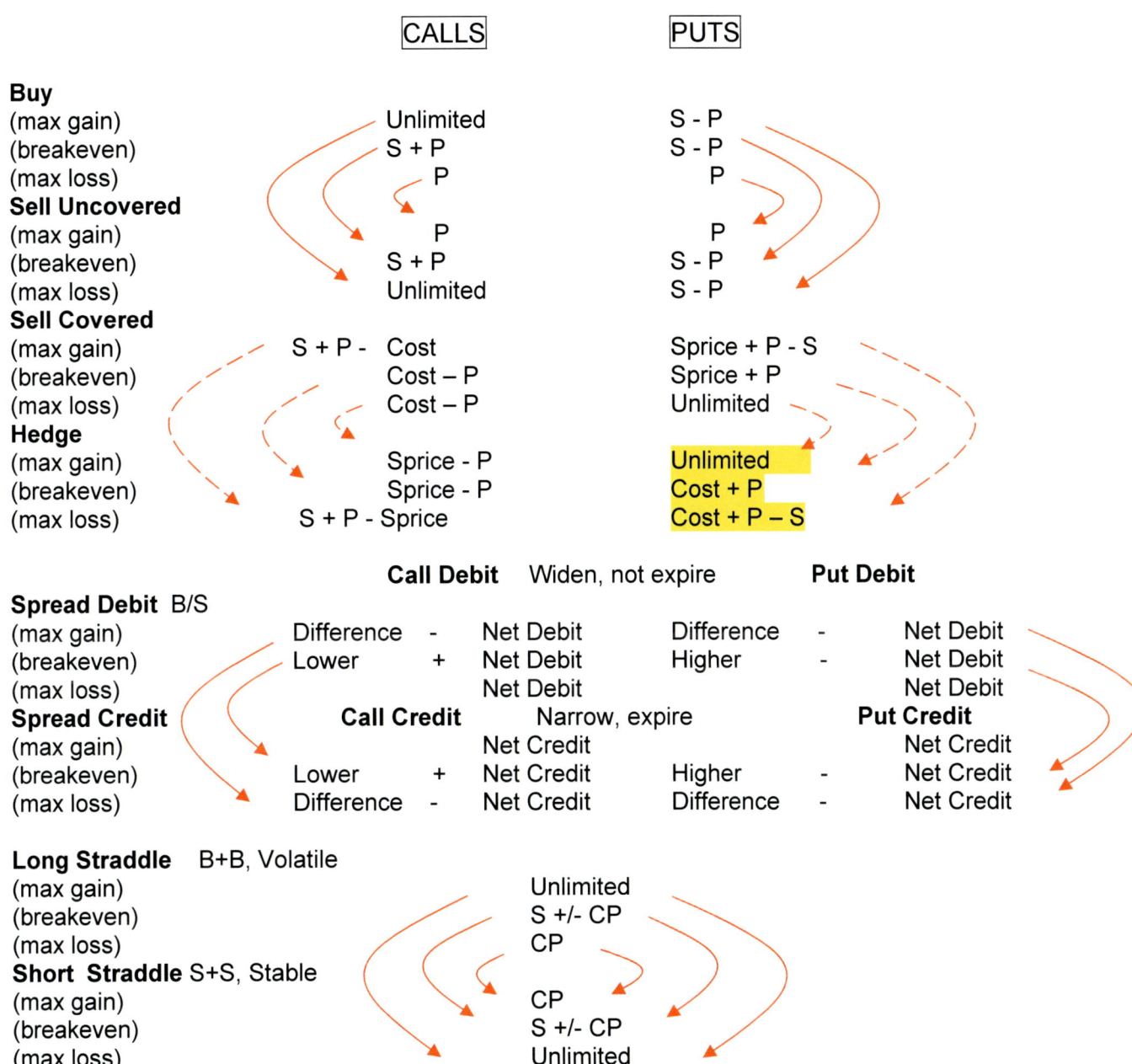

	CALLS	PUTS
Buy		
(max gain)	Unlimited	S - P
(breakeven)	S + P	S - P
(max loss)	P	P
Sell Uncovered		
(max gain)	P	P
(breakeven)	S + P	S - P
(max loss)	Unlimited	S - P
Sell Covered		
(max gain)	S + P - Cost	Sprice + P - S
(breakeven)	Cost – P	Sprice + P
(max loss)	Cost – P	Unlimited
Hedge		
(max gain)	Sprice - P	Unlimited
(breakeven)	Sprice - P	Cost + P
(max loss)	S + P - Sprice	Cost + P – S

	Call Debit	Widen, not expire	**Put Debit**	
Spread Debit B/S				
(max gain)	Difference - Net Debit		Difference - Net Debit	
(breakeven)	Lower + Net Debit		Higher - Net Debit	
(max loss)	Net Debit		Net Debit	
Spread Credit	**Call Credit**	Narrow, expire	**Put Credit**	
(max gain)	Net Credit		Net Credit	
(breakeven)	Lower + Net Credit		Higher - Net Credit	
(max loss)	Difference - Net Credit		Difference - Net Credit	

Long Straddle B+B, Volatile
(max gain) Unlimited
(breakeven) S +/- CP
(max loss) CP

Short Straddle S+S, Stable
(max gain) CP
(breakeven) S +/- CP
(max loss) Unlimited

Question: An investor sells short 100 shares of ABC and buys an ABC call for a premium of $4.
Thought: It's a purchase of a call, and he is short the stock. The investor is hedging the stock with an options purchase. He's short with a call. Section 4 of the chart.

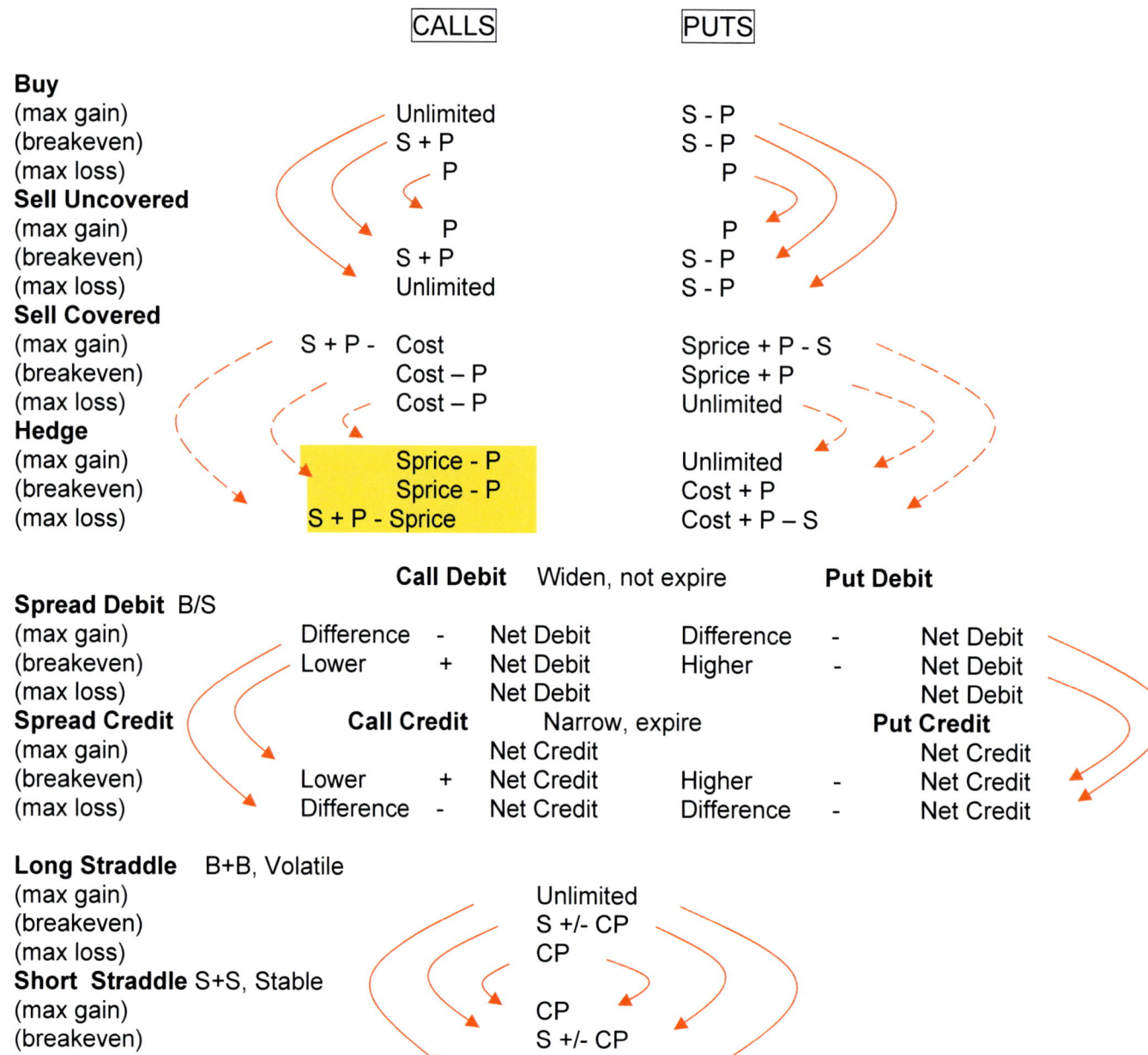

Question: An investor buys one ABC June 30 call for $1 and sells one June 25 ABC call for $6... **Thought:** It's a buy/sell combo on calls making this a call spread. He paid $1 and received $6, making it a credit spread. It's a call credit spread. Section 6 of the chart.

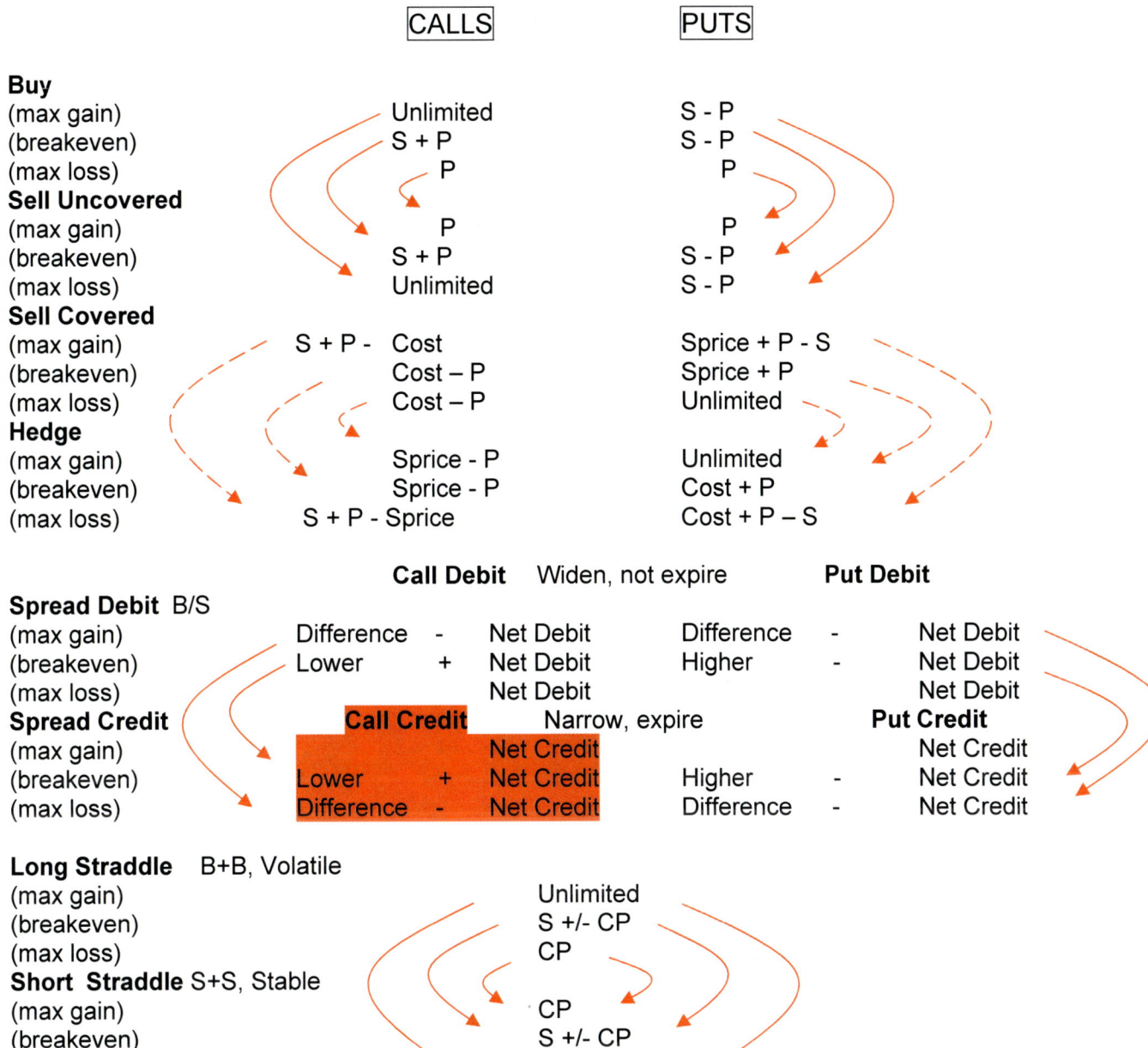

Question: An investor buys one ABC call and buys one ABC put... **Thought:** It's a buy/buy on a call/put. The buy/buy makes this a long straddle. Section 7 of the chart.

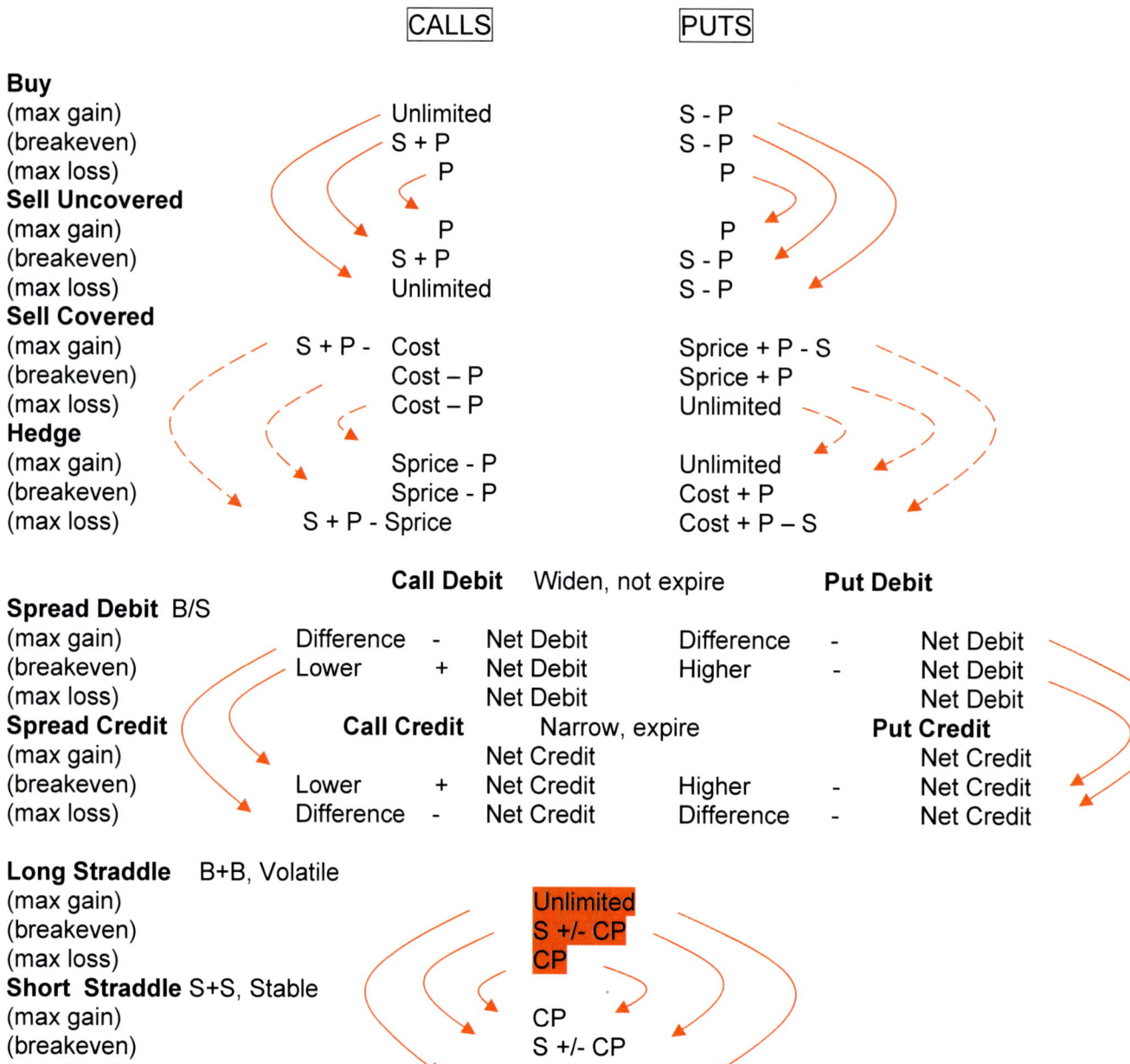

> Here is the thought process applied to simulated exam questions:

A customer buys an ABC June 40 put when the market price of ABC is also $40 per share and pays a premium of 3. What is the customer's maximum risk? The customer bought a put, section 1, max loss = premium. 3.

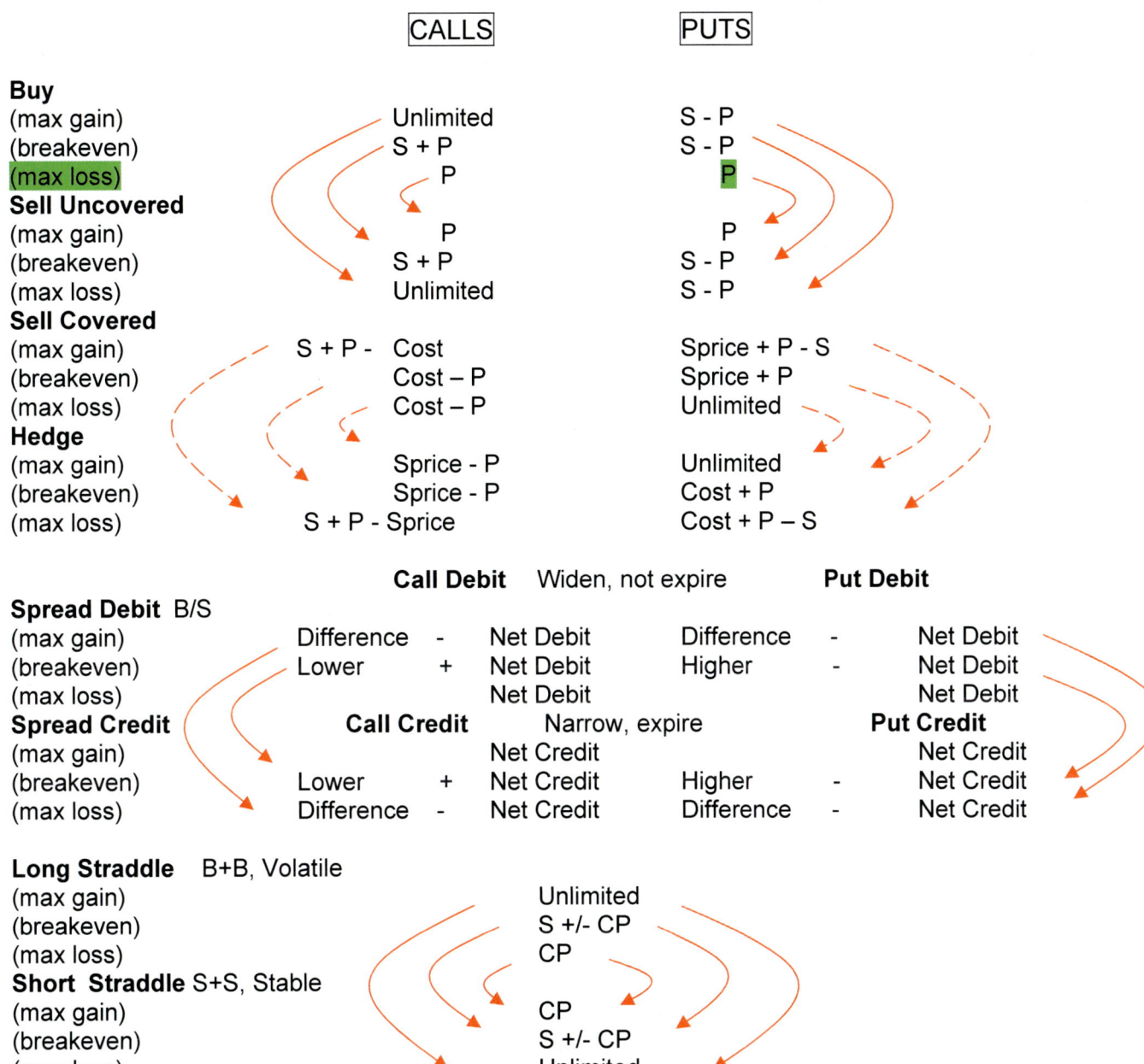

A customer buys ten September 60 calls and pays a $3 premium on each call. The current market price of ABC is $58 per share. What would the investor's breakeven point be? The customer bought calls, section 1, breakeven = strike + premium. 60 + 3 = 63.

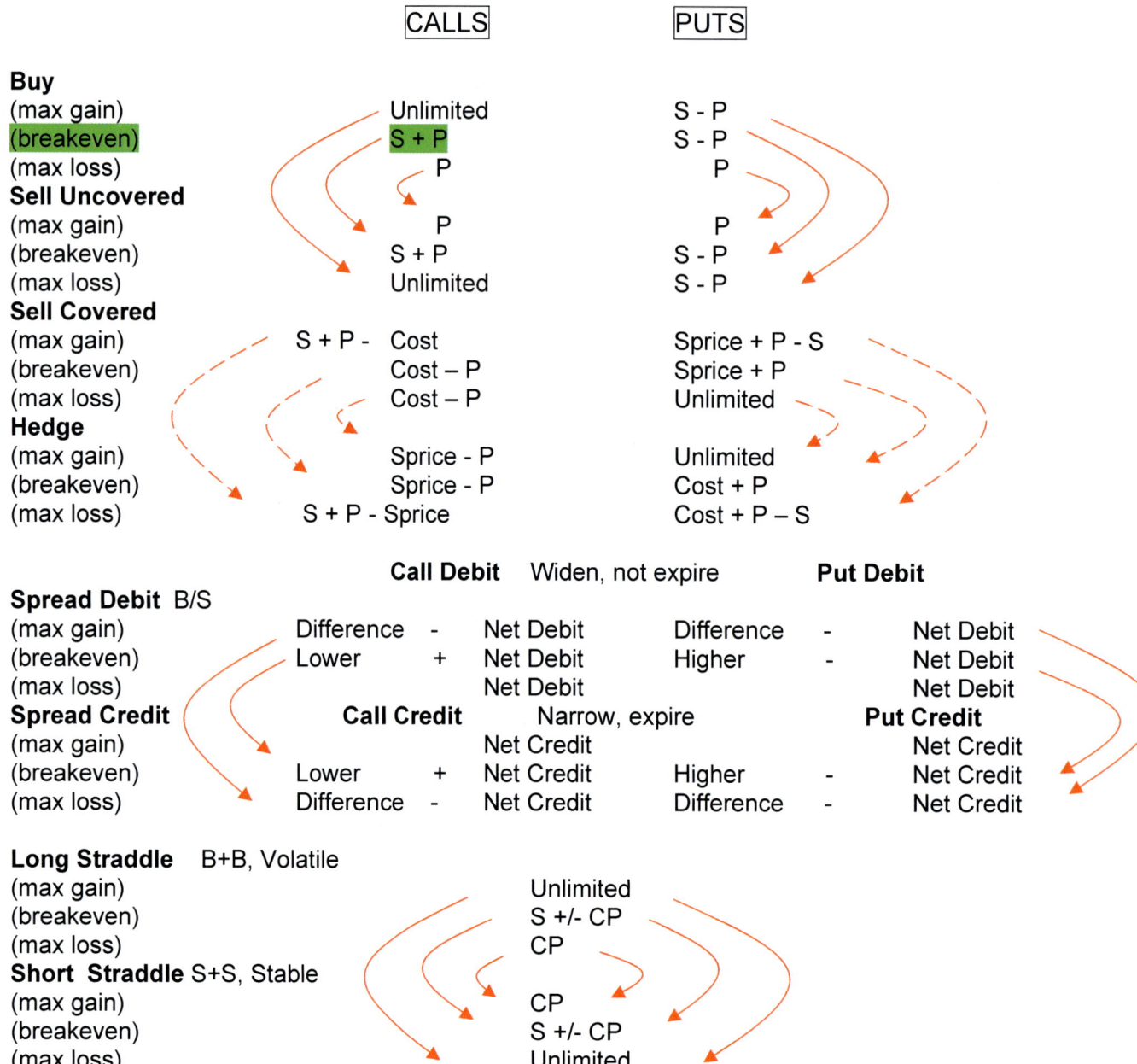

	CALLS	PUTS
Buy		
(max gain)	Unlimited	S - P
(breakeven)	S + P	S - P
(max loss)	P	P
Sell Uncovered		
(max gain)	P	P
(breakeven)	S + P	S - P
(max loss)	Unlimited	S - P
Sell Covered		
(max gain)	S + P - Cost	Sprice + P - S
(breakeven)	Cost – P	Sprice + P
(max loss)	Cost – P	Unlimited
Hedge		
(max gain)	Sprice - P	Unlimited
(breakeven)	Sprice - P	Cost + P
(max loss)	S + P - Sprice	Cost + P – S

	Call Debit	Widen, not expire	Put Debit	
Spread Debit B/S				
(max gain)	Difference - Net Debit		Difference - Net Debit	
(breakeven)	Lower + Net Debit		Higher - Net Debit	
(max loss)	Net Debit		Net Debit	
Spread Credit	Call Credit	Narrow, expire	Put Credit	
(max gain)	Net Credit		Net Credit	
(breakeven)	Lower + Net Credit		Higher - Net Credit	
(max loss)	Difference - Net Credit		Difference - Net Credit	

Long Straddle B+B, Volatile
(max gain)   Unlimited
(breakeven)   S +/- CP
(max loss)   CP
Short Straddle S+S, Stable
(max gain)   CP
(breakeven)   S +/- CP
(max loss)   Unlimited

An investor buys 100 shares of ABC at $30 per share and at the same time writes an ABC 30 call option for a $5 premium. At what price would ABC have to be selling for the writer to break even? The investor bought stock and sold a call – he's covered call writing. Section three. The breakeven point is the cost of the stock – premium. 30 – 5 = 25.

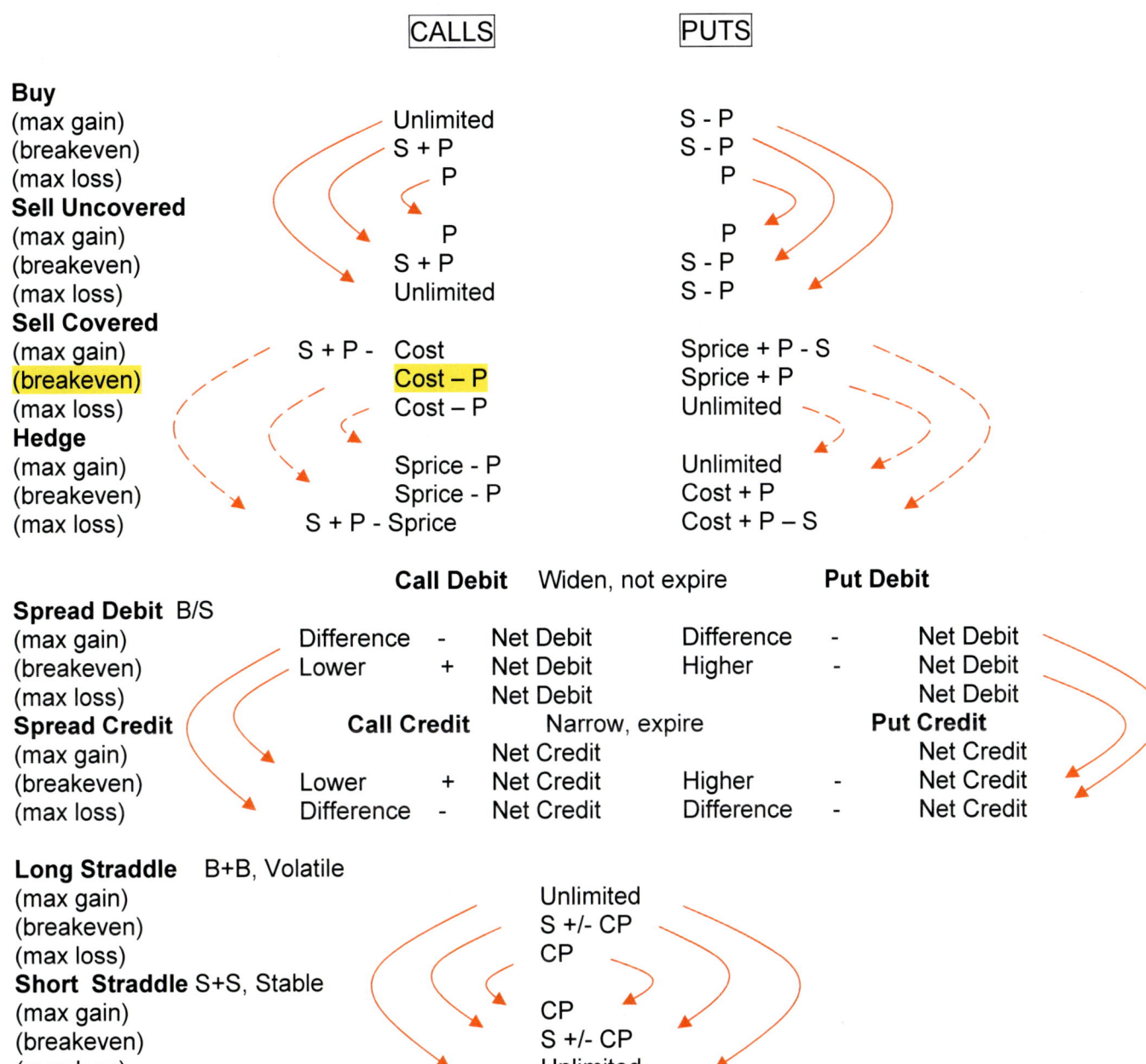

A customer buys 100 shares of ABC at $42 per share. The customer is on the golf course and hears talk of an impending bear market. The customer calls his broker and buys an ABC March 40 put for a 2 point premium. What is the maximum loss potential for this customer? This is a customer that owns stock and he bought a put. It's a hedge against the stock going down. Section 4. The max loss for stock with a put is cost + p – s. 42 +2 – 40 = 4.

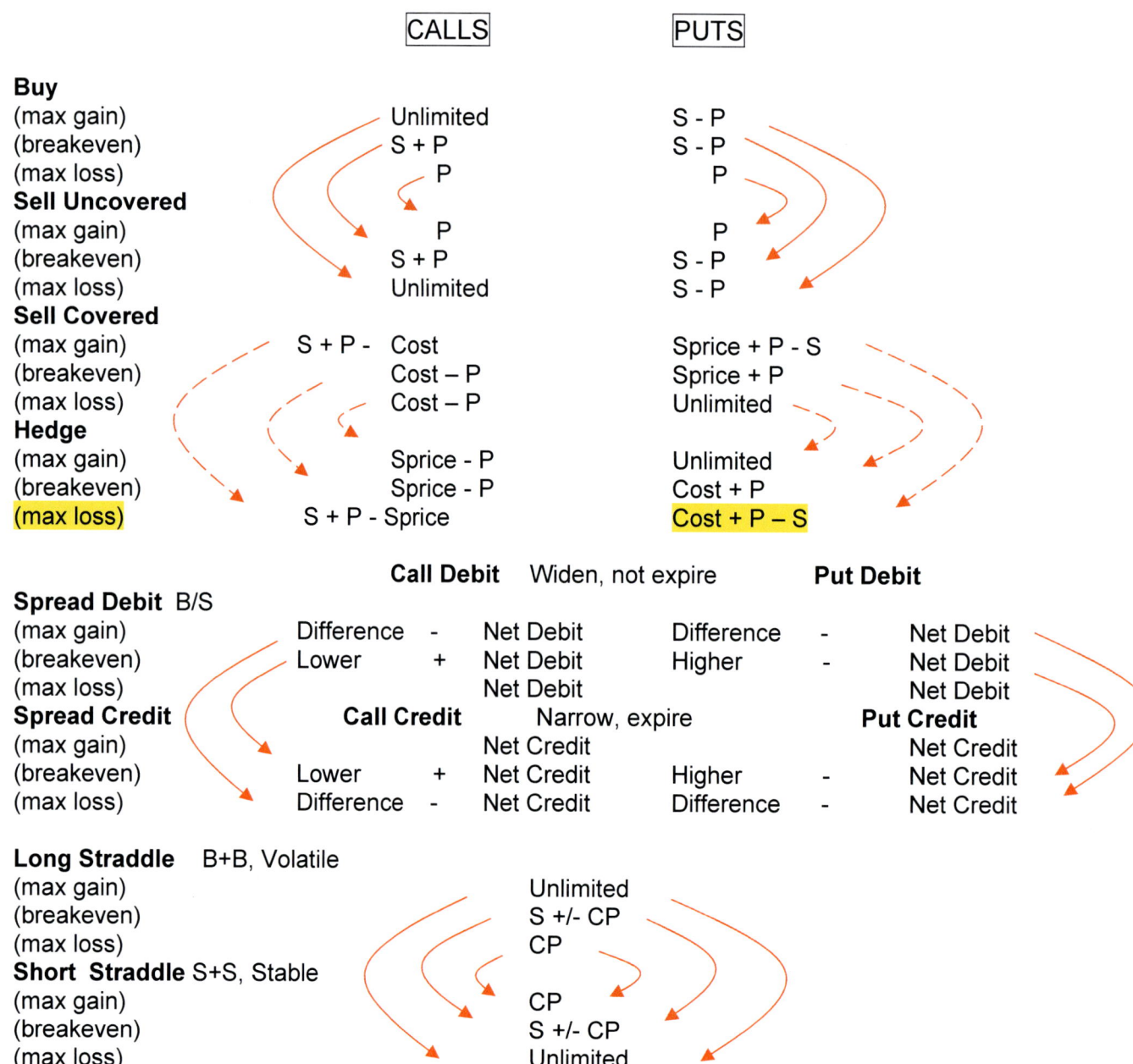

An investor buys an XYZ July 50 call and an XYZ July 50 put. This is an example of_____? The investor is "buying and buying" a call/put combo. It's a long straddle. If he were "selling and selling" a call/put combo it would be a short straddle. Section 7 shows the "B+B" hint signifying a buy and a buy.

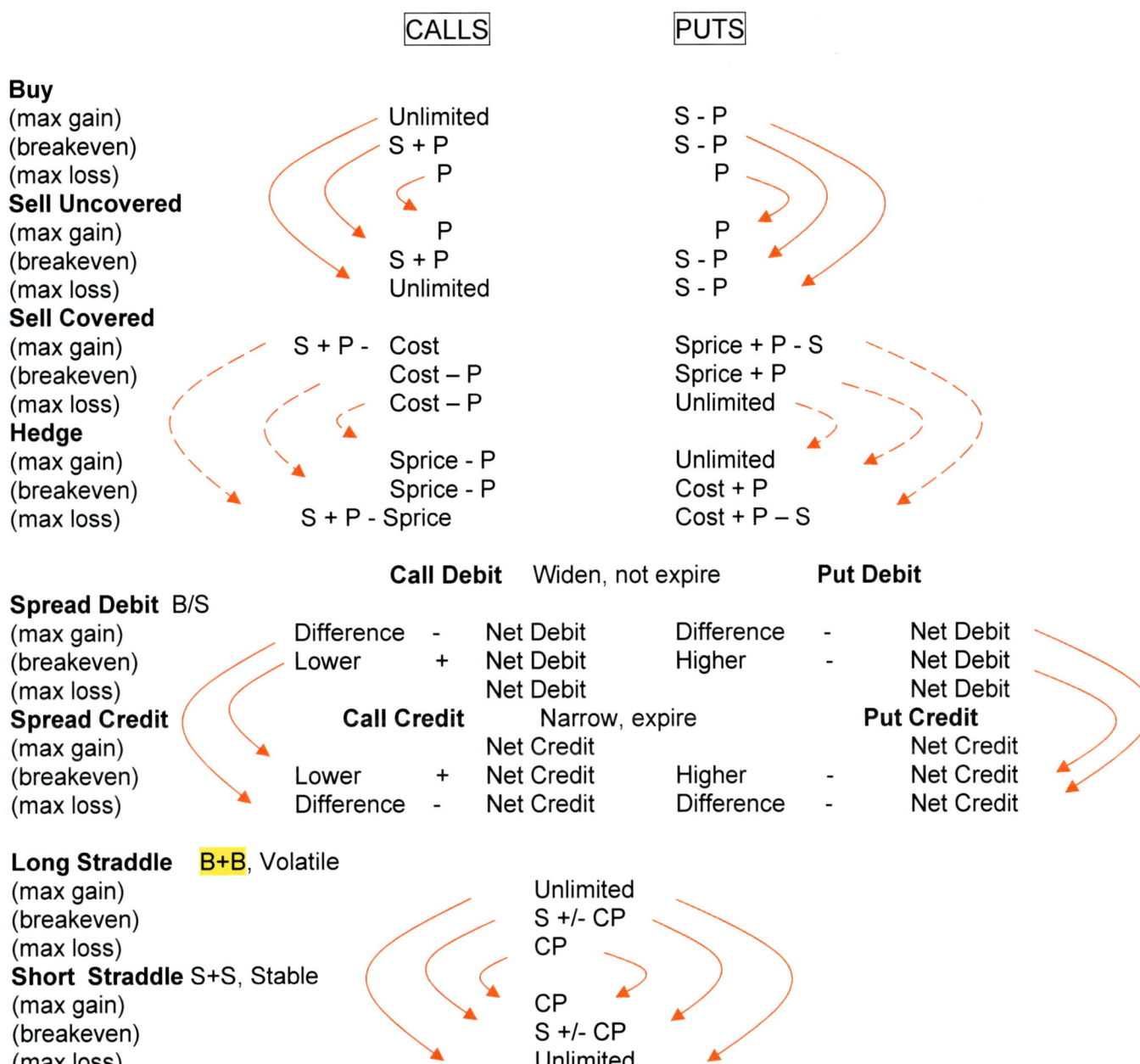

A customer sells one XYZ March 20 put for a premium of $3. At what market price will the customer break even? What is the maximum loss that the customer could realize? What is the maximum possible profit? The customer sold a put and the question does not mention a stock position in conjunction with this put, so I believe it to be a uncovered sale of a put. Therefore, I look at section two and see that the breakeven would be the strike price – premium. 20 – 3 = 17. Max loss is also 20 – 3 = 17. Max profit is the premium of 3.

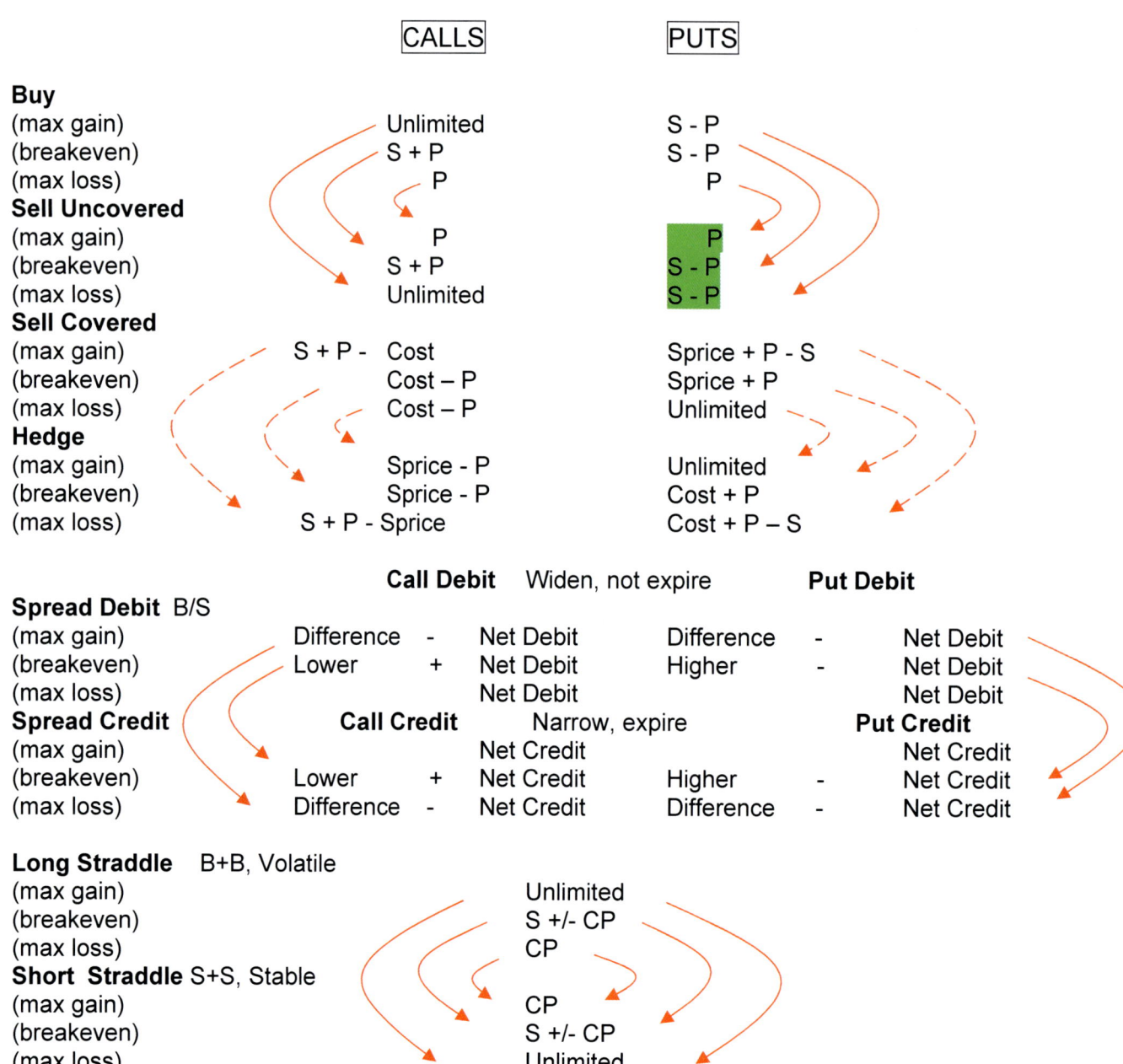

A customer buys 1 ABC August 70 put for 4 and 1 ABC August 70 call for 4. The price of ABC stock is $70. For the customer to break even, the stock would have to be selling at what price?
Again, the customer is "buying and buying". This is a long straddle. There are going to be two breakeven points. The strike price + the combined premium, and the strike price – the combined premium. The strike price is 70 and the premiums add to 8. The breakeven points are 70 + 8 = 78 and 70 – 8 = 62.

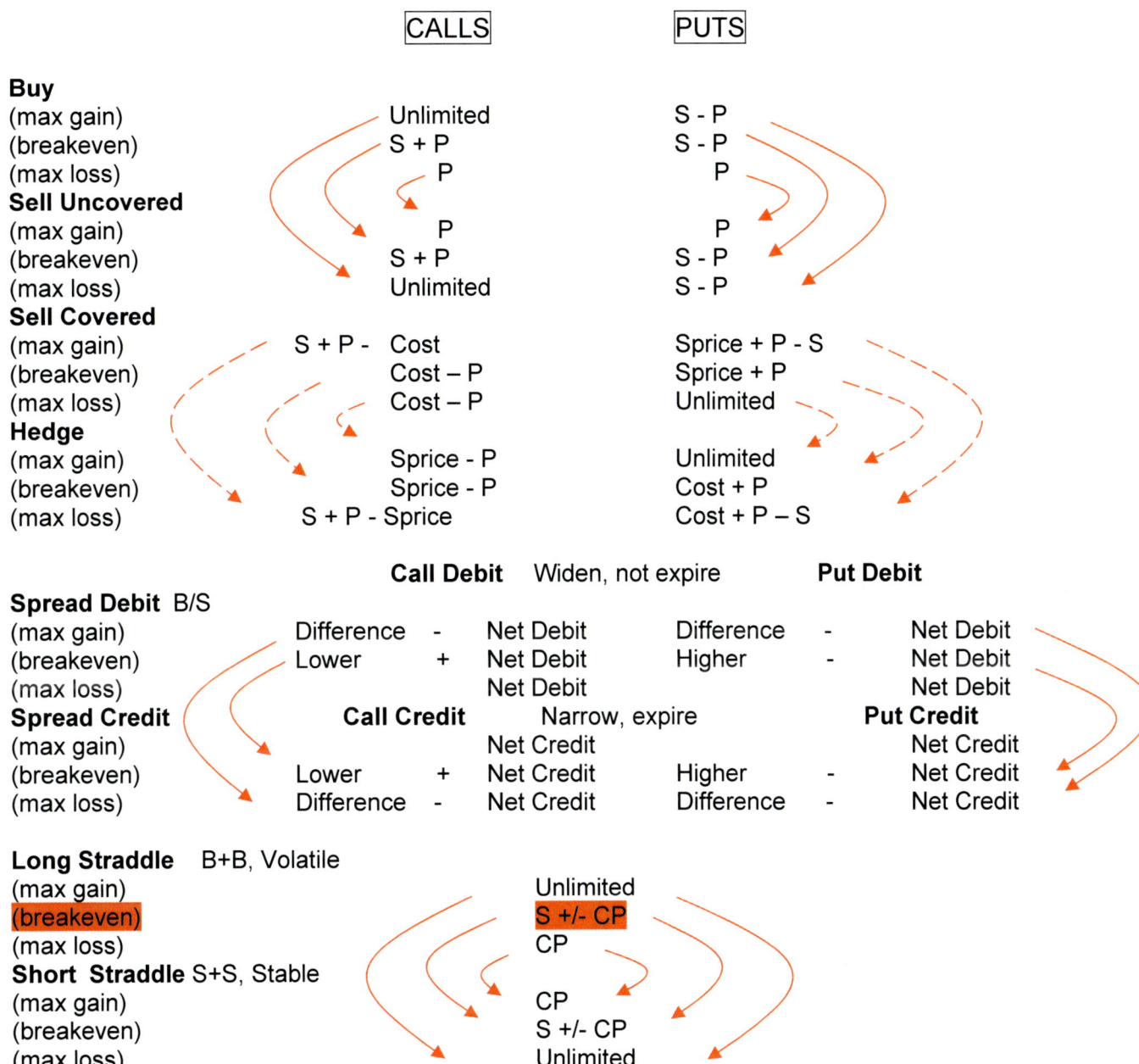

A customer with no other positions sells an ABC July 70 call for 6 and buys 100 shares of ABC stock for 65 per share. At what price will the customer break even? The investor bought stock and sold a call – he's covered call writing. Section three. The breakeven point is the cost of the stock – premium. 65 - 6 = 59.

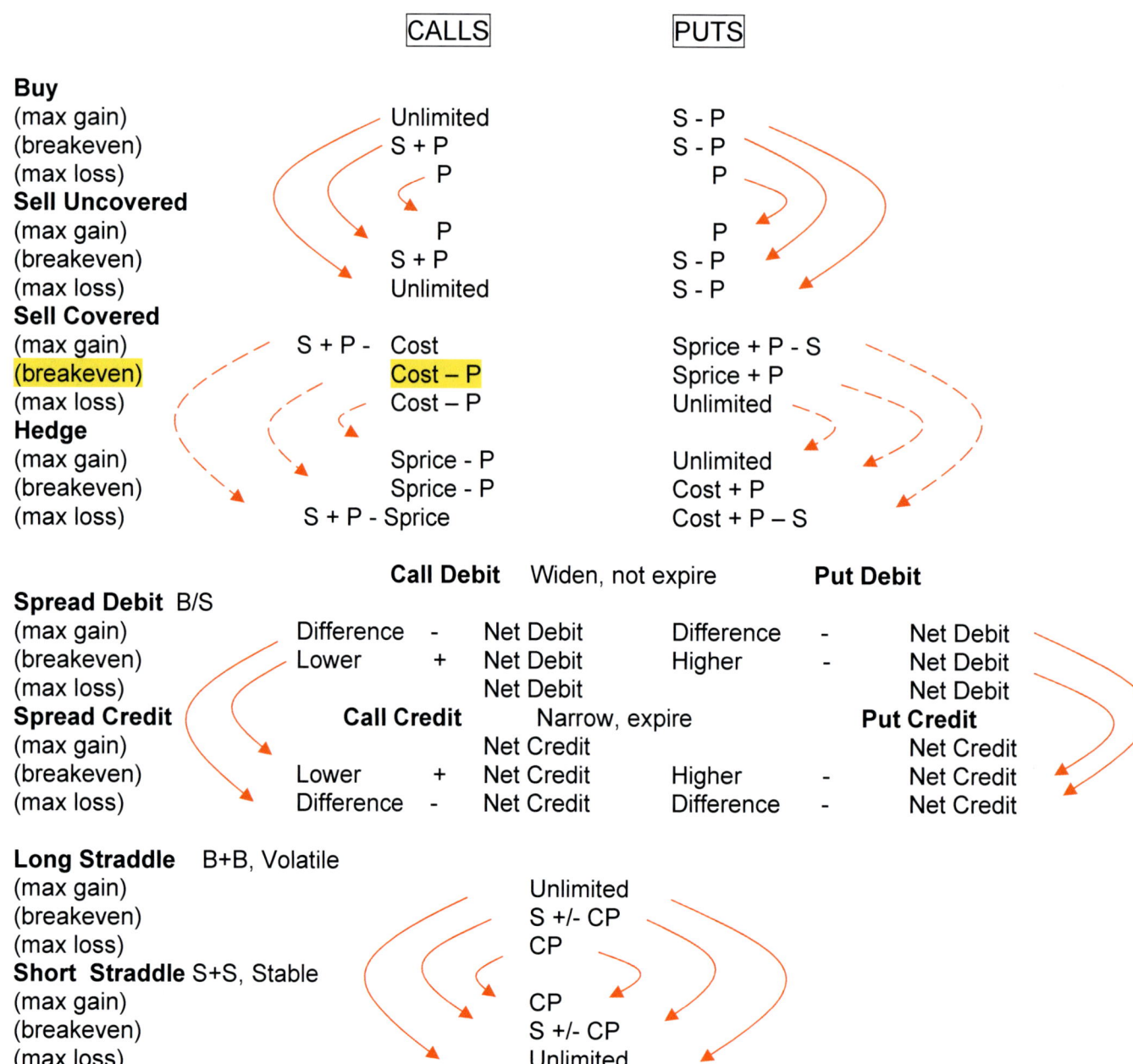

	CALLS	**PUTS**
Buy		
(max gain)	Unlimited	S - P
(breakeven)	S + P	S - P
(max loss)	P	P
Sell Uncovered		
(max gain)	P	P
(breakeven)	S + P	S - P
(max loss)	Unlimited	S - P
Sell Covered		
(max gain)	S + P - Cost	Sprice + P - S
(breakeven)	Cost – P	Sprice + P
(max loss)	Cost – P	Unlimited
Hedge		
(max gain)	Sprice - P	Unlimited
(breakeven)	Sprice - P	Cost + P
(max loss)	S + P - Sprice	Cost + P – S

	Call Debit	Widen, not expire	**Put Debit**	
Spread Debit B/S				
(max gain)	Difference -	Net Debit	Difference -	Net Debit
(breakeven)	Lower +	Net Debit	Higher -	Net Debit
(max loss)		Net Debit		Net Debit
Spread Credit	**Call Credit**	Narrow, expire	**Put Credit**	
(max gain)		Net Credit		Net Credit
(breakeven)	Lower +	Net Credit	Higher -	Net Credit
(max loss)	Difference -	Net Credit	Difference -	Net Credit

Long Straddle B+B, Volatile
(max gain) Unlimited
(breakeven) S +/- CP
(max loss) CP

Short Straddle S+S, Stable
(max gain) CP
(breakeven) S +/- CP
(max loss) Unlimited

An investor buys 1 XYZ January 60 call at 6 and writes 1 XYZ January 70 call at 2. What is the investor's maximum potential loss? What is the investor's breakeven point? What is the investor's maximum potential gain? The investor is "buying and selling". A buy/sell combo with options is a spread. He paid 6 and received 2, so it's a debit of 4. Section 5 deals with debit spreads. The calls are on the left. It's a call debit spread. Max gain is the difference in strikes – the net debit. 10 is the difference in strikes, so the formula is 10 – 4 = 6. The breakeven point is the lower strike price + the net debit. 60 + 4 = 64. The max loss is the net debit of 4.

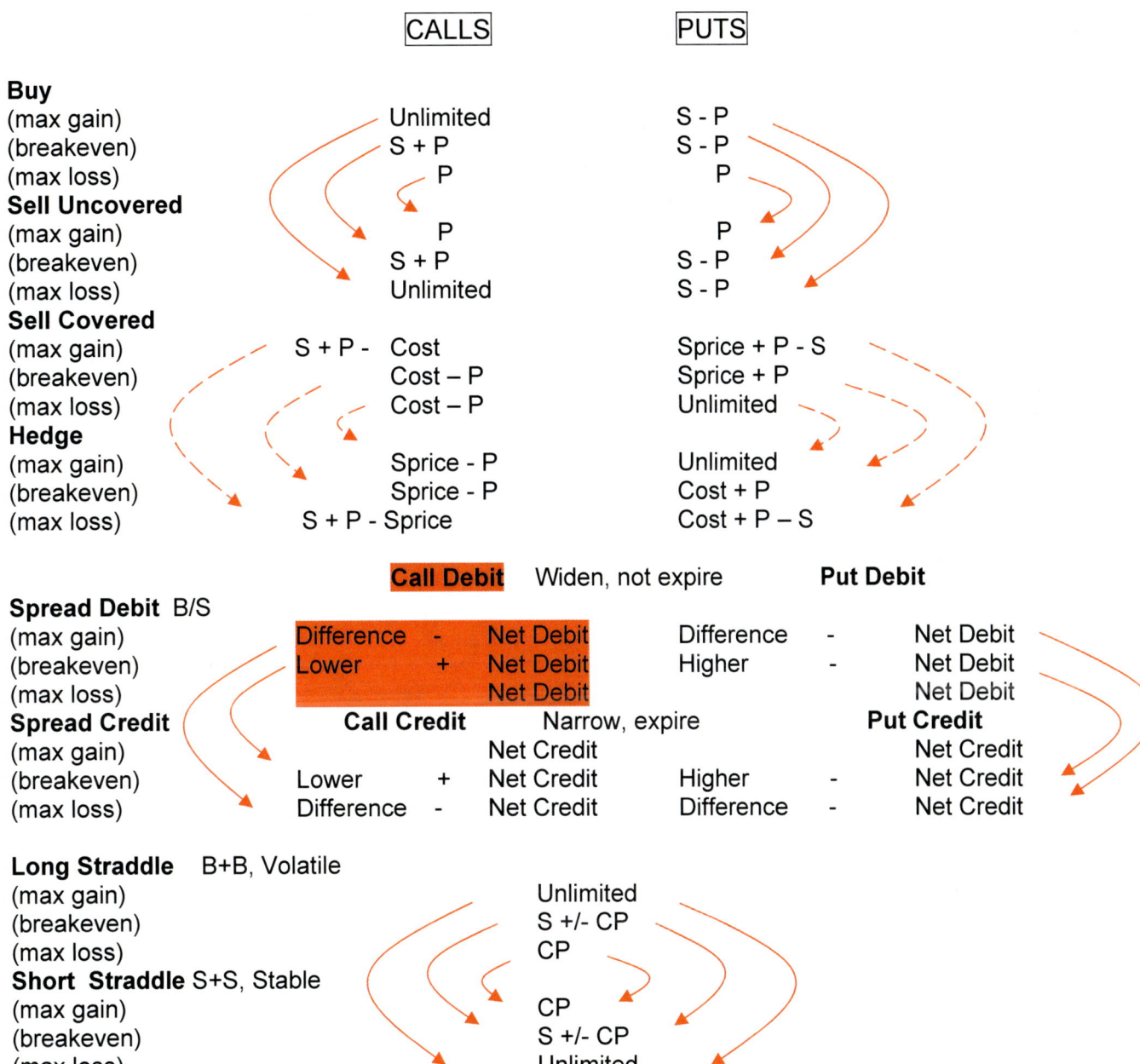

An investor bought an XYZ September 70 put at 1 and wrote 1 XYZ September 80 put at 8. Max profit? Breakeven? Max loss? Does the investor wish to see the spread widen or narrow? The investor has a buy/sell combo making this a spread. He's buying and selling puts, so it's a put spread. He sold for 8 and only paid 1, so he has a credit of 7 making this a put credit spread. Max gain is net credit, which is 7. Breakeven point would be the higher strike minus the net credit, which is 80 – 7 = 73. The max loss would be the difference – the net credit, which is 10 – 7 = 3. The hint on the chart next to the net credits shows that the investor would like the spread to narrow.

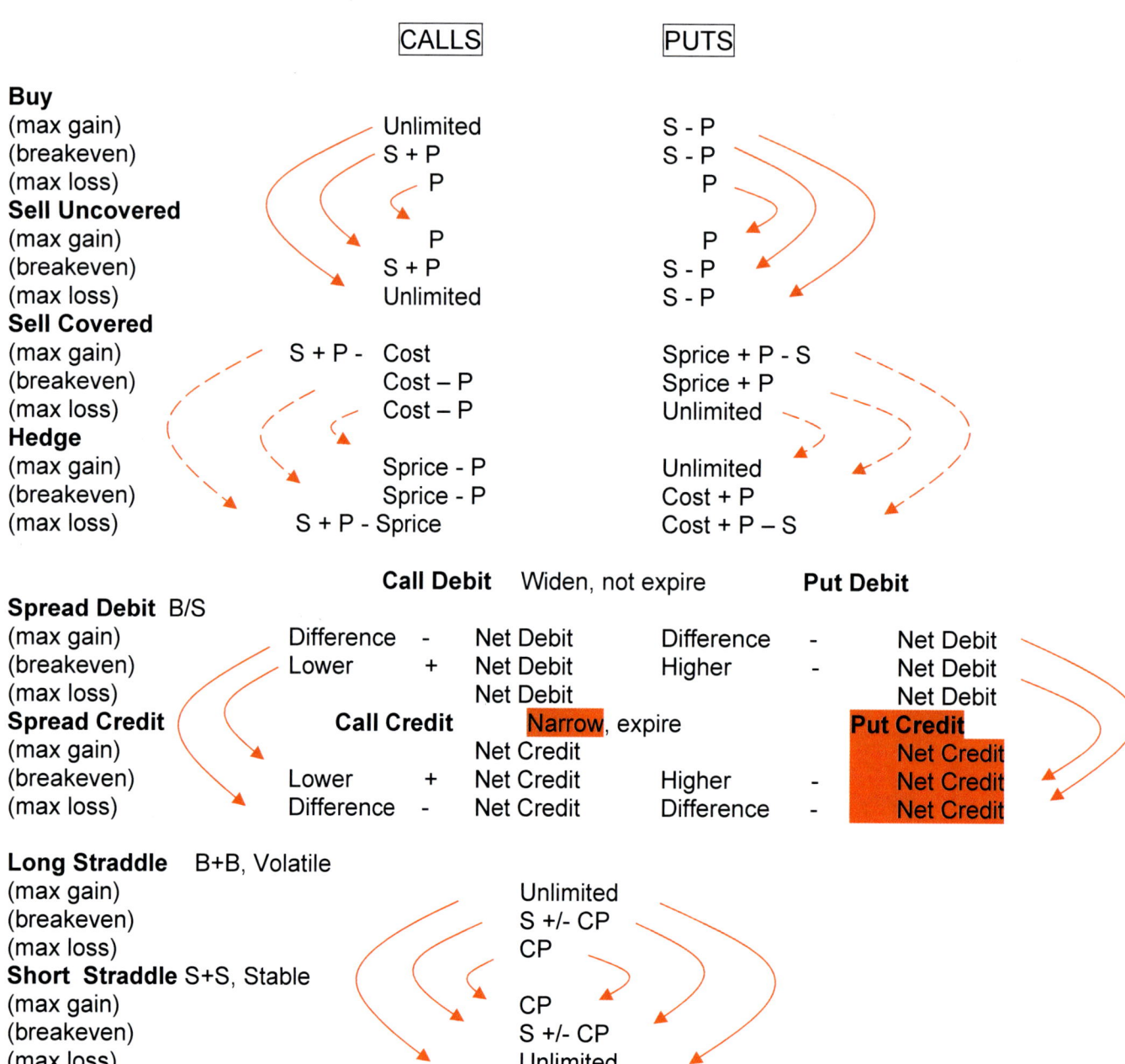

		CALLS	PUTS
Buy			
(max gain)		Unlimited	S - P
(breakeven)		S + P	S - P
(max loss)		P	P
Sell Uncovered			
(max gain)		P	P
(breakeven)		S + P	S - P
(max loss)		Unlimited	S - P
Sell Covered			
(max gain)	S + P -	Cost	Sprice + P - S
(breakeven)		Cost – P	Sprice + P
(max loss)		Cost – P	Unlimited
Hedge			
(max gain)		Sprice - P	Unlimited
(breakeven)		Sprice - P	Cost + P
(max loss)		S + P - Sprice	Cost + P – S
	Call Debit	Widen, not expire	**Put Debit**
Spread Debit B/S			
(max gain)	Difference -	Net Debit	Difference - Net Debit
(breakeven)	Lower +	Net Debit	Higher - Net Debit
(max loss)		Net Debit	Net Debit
Spread Credit	**Call Credit**	Narrow, expire	**Put Credit**
(max gain)		Net Credit	Net Credit
(breakeven)	Lower +	Net Credit	Higher - Net Credit
(max loss)	Difference -	Net Credit	Difference - Net Credit
Long Straddle B+B, Volatile			
(max gain)		Unlimited	
(breakeven)		S +/- CP	
(max loss)		CP	
Short Straddle S+S, Stable			
(max gain)		CP	
(breakeven)		S +/- CP	
(max loss)		Unlimited	

THE AUDIO FILE TO ACCOMPANY THIS BOOK IS AVAILABLE AT FACEBOOK.COM/SOYOUFLUNKEDTHESERIES7EXAM

Please try finding the answers to the following questions on your own. Read the question, and try to determine where on the chart the strategy is found.

Question: "An investor writes one ABC Feb 20 put for a premium of $2". What is the breakeven point"?

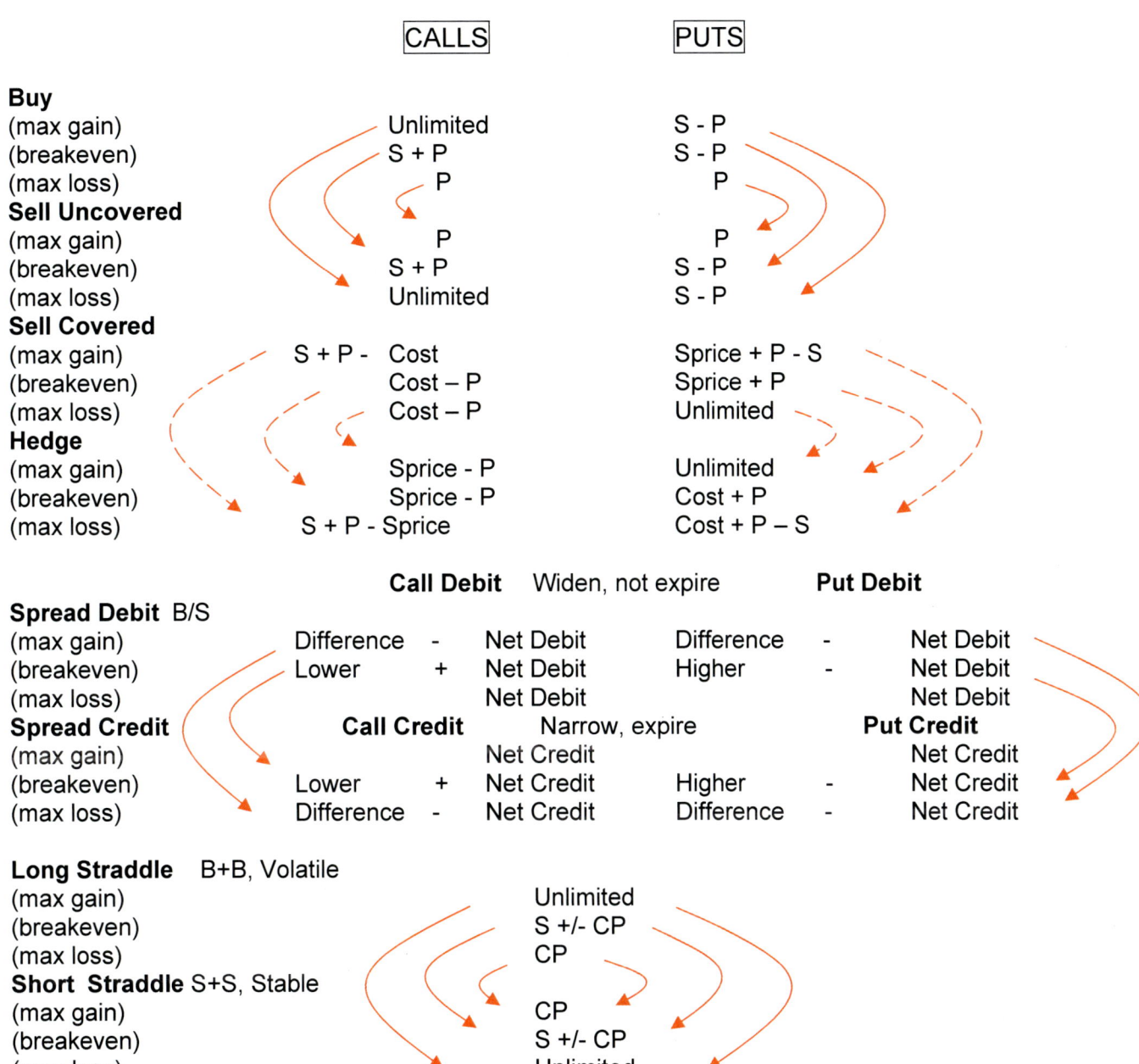

Question: "A customer buys ten listed ABC Corporation Jan 60 calls and pays a $7 premium per contract. The current price of the stock is also $60 per share." What is the maximum possible loss"?

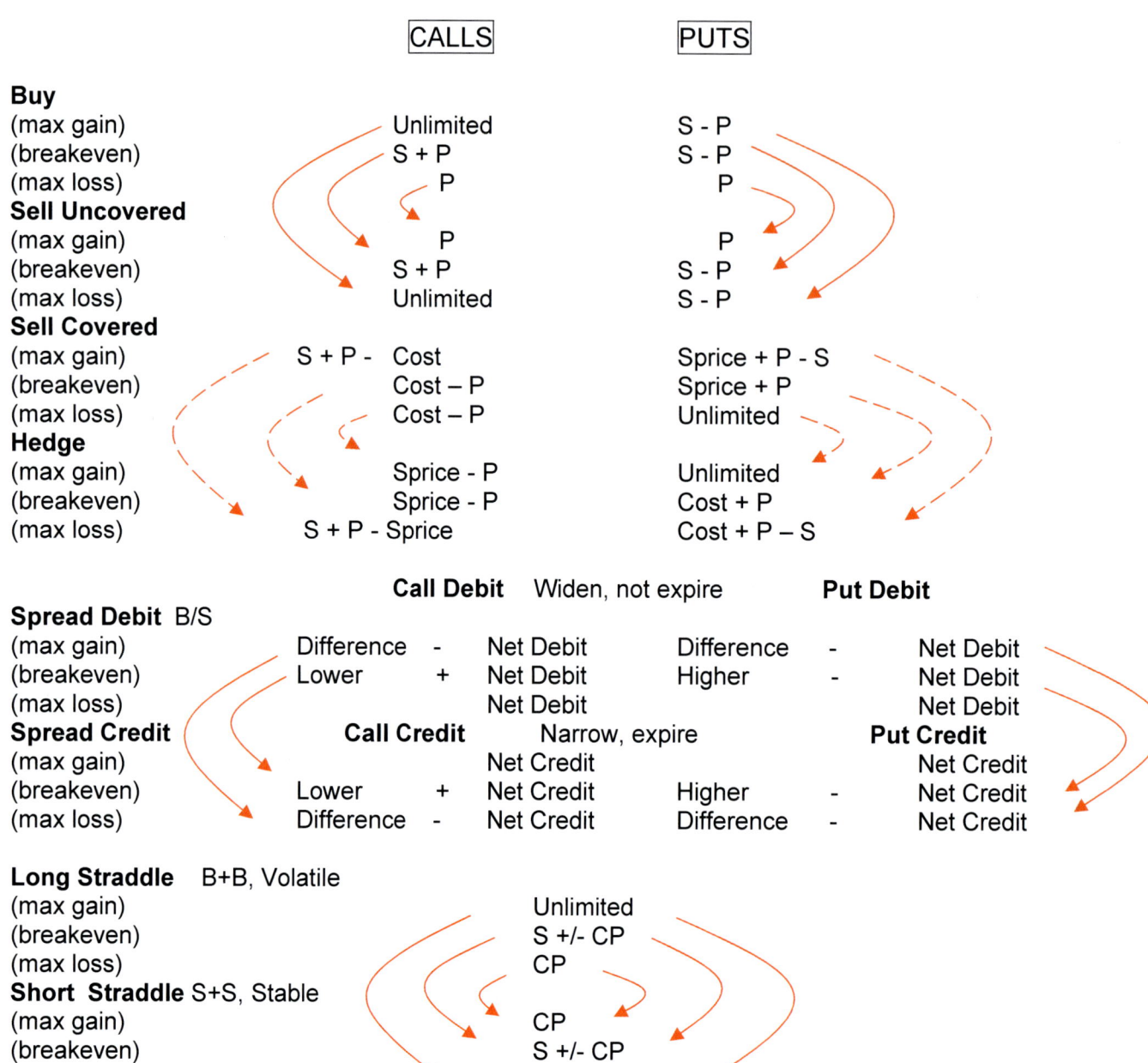

Question: An investor sells short 100 shares of ABC at 52 and also sells one ABC 50 put for a $3 premium". What is the maximum profit and maximum loss"?

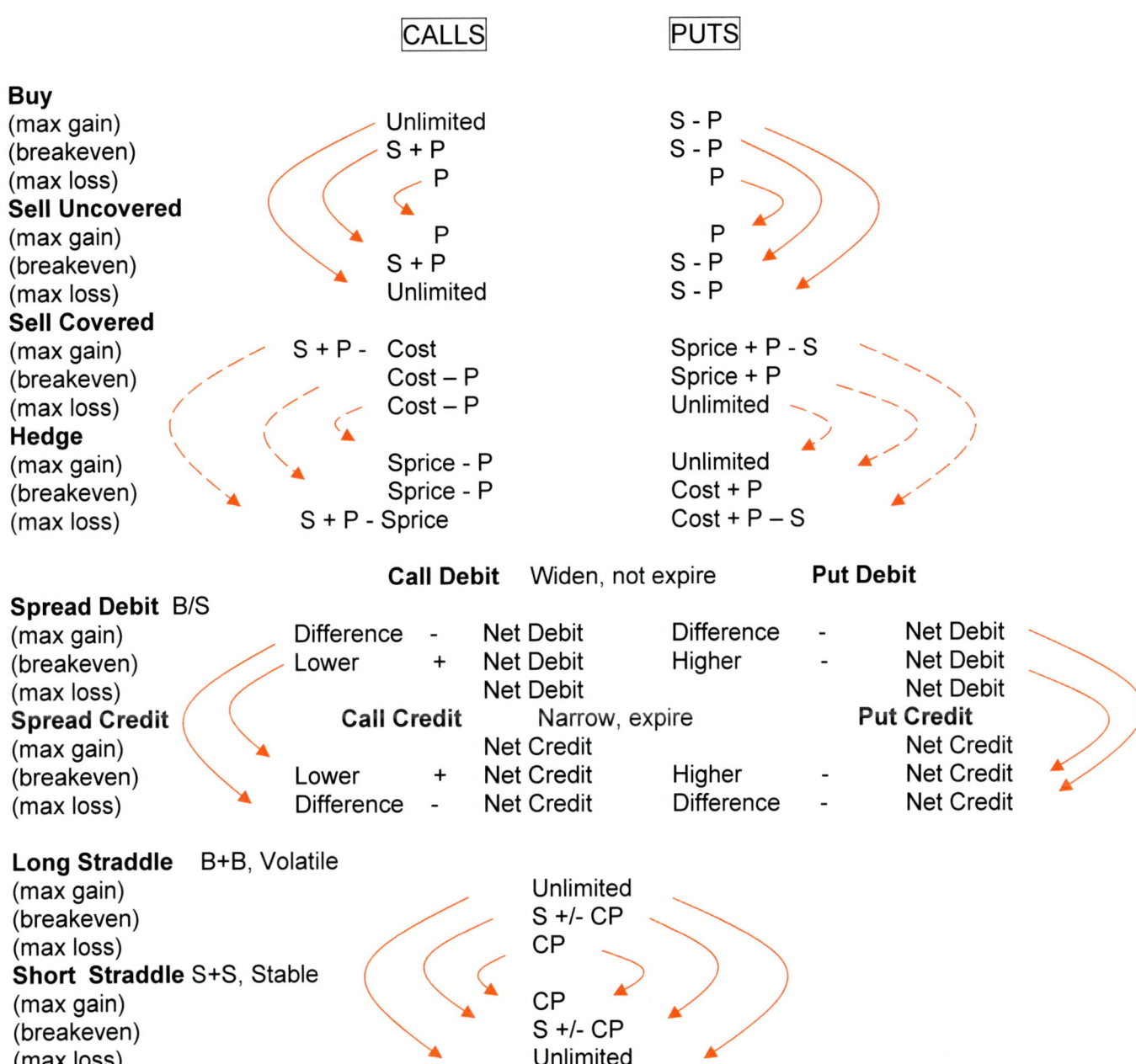

THE AUDIO FILE TO ACCOMPANY THIS BOOK IS AVAILABLE AT FACEBOOK.COM/SOYOUFLUNKEDTHESERIES7EXAM

Question: "A customer buys 15 XYZ June 45 calls at 4 and buys 15 XYZ June 45 puts at 4". What is the maximum possible gain for this position? The maximum possible loss? The breakeven?

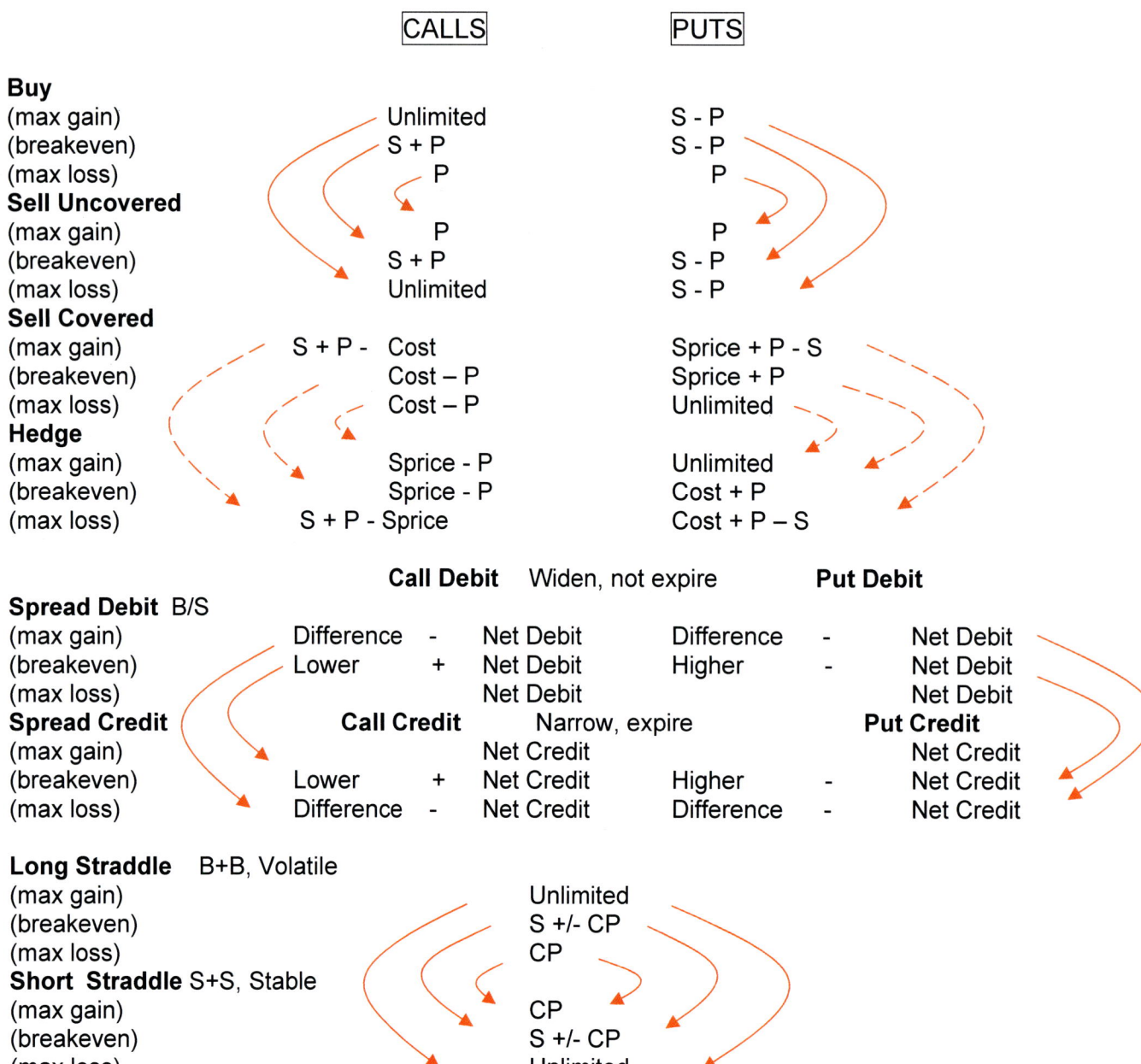

Question: "An investor buys 1 ABC June 30 call at 1 and writes 1 ABC June 25 call at 3". Does the investor desire the spread to narrow or widen? Does the investor desire the calls to expire"?

	CALLS	PUTS
Buy		
(max gain)	Unlimited	S - P
(breakeven)	S + P	S - P
(max loss)	P	P
Sell Uncovered		
(max gain)	P	P
(breakeven)	S + P	S - P
(max loss)	Unlimited	S - P
Sell Covered		
(max gain)	S + P - Cost	Sprice + P - S
(breakeven)	Cost – P	Sprice + P
(max loss)	Cost – P	Unlimited
Hedge		
(max gain)	Sprice - P	Unlimited
(breakeven)	Sprice - P	Cost + P
(max loss)	S + P - Sprice	Cost + P – S

	Call Debit	Widen, not expire	**Put Debit**	
Spread Debit B/S				
(max gain)	Difference - Net Debit		Difference - Net Debit	
(breakeven)	Lower + Net Debit		Higher - Net Debit	
(max loss)	Net Debit		Net Debit	
Spread Credit	**Call Credit**	Narrow, expire	**Put Credit**	
(max gain)	Net Credit		Net Credit	
(breakeven)	Lower + Net Credit		Higher - Net Credit	
(max loss)	Difference - Net Credit		Difference - Net Credit	

Long Straddle B+B, Volatile
(max gain)   Unlimited
(breakeven)   S +/- CP
(max loss)   CP

Short Straddle S+S, Stable
(max gain)   CP
(breakeven)   S +/- CP
(max loss)   Unlimited

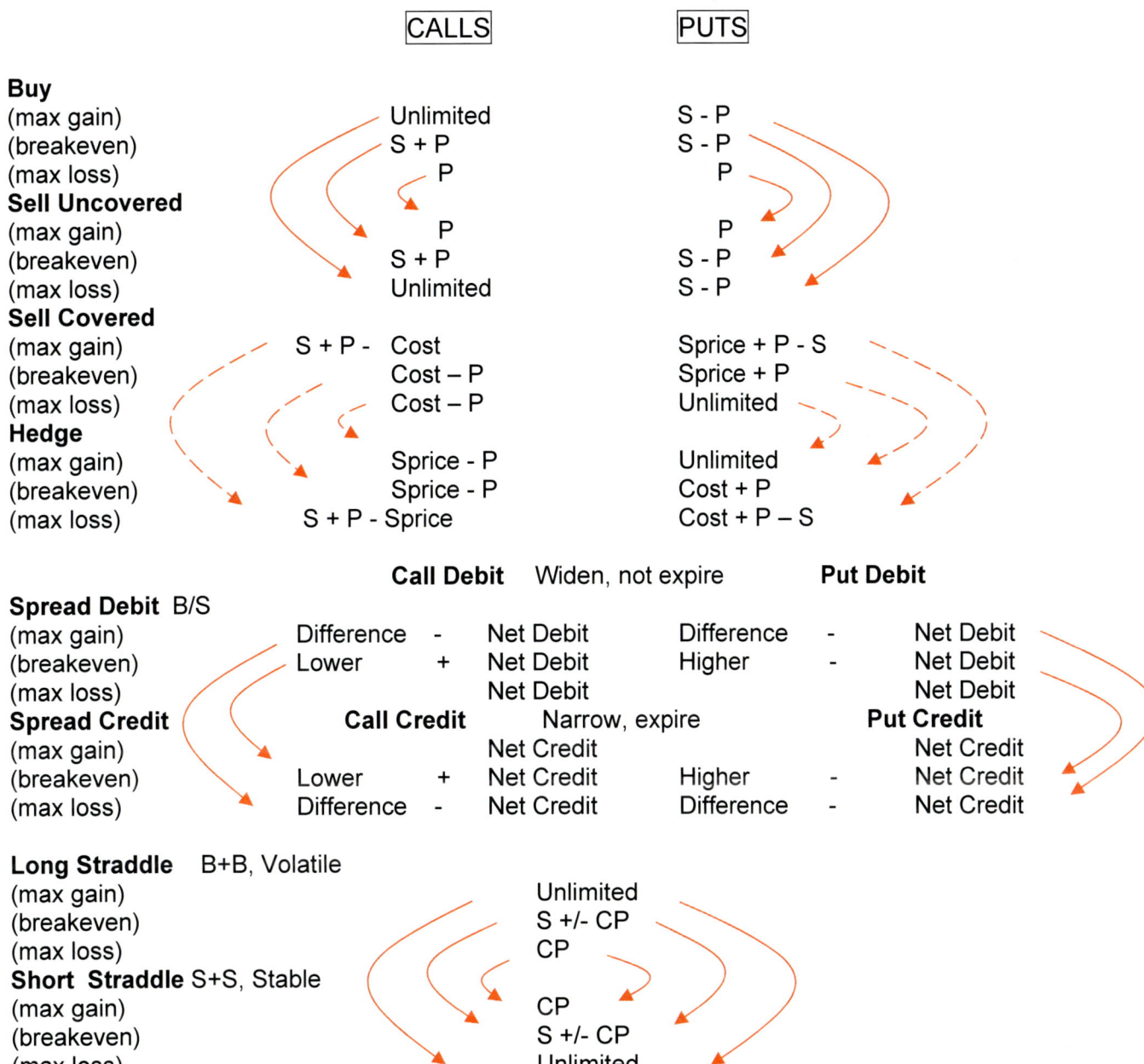

THE AUDIO FILE TO ACCOMPANY THIS BOOK IS AVAILABLE AT FACEBOOK.COM/SOYOUFLUNKEDTHESERIES7EXAM

THE MINI CHARTS

As stated earlier, you will come across questions that must be completely thought out. Shown below are two simple charts that are very helpful when you are concentrating on the mechanics of options questions. Also, a "money box" is helpful to track the flow of funds.

Bullish vs. Bearish:

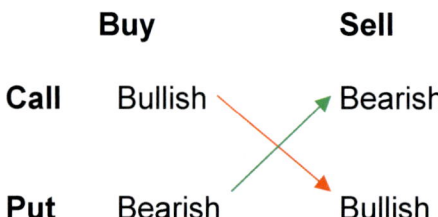

	Buy	**Sell**
Call	Bullish	Bearish
Put	Bearish	Bullish

To determine if a spread is bullish or bearish, simply look to the strike prices-If you are long the lower strike price, you are bullish. "Long the lower" = Bullish. Here is an example:

Buy 1 ABC March 50 put
Sell 1 ABC March 60 put

This is a bullish position due to the lower strike price of 50 being long. Note that it is irrelevant whether the contracts are calls or puts, or if there is a net debit or net credit. "Long the lower" will reveal a bullish position.

Rights vs. Obligations:

	Buy	**Sell**
Call	Right to buy stock	Obligated to sell stock
Put	Right to sell stock	Obligated to buy stock

The Money Box:

An example of a question that has to be thought out would be something such as this: An investor purchases 1 ABC March 60 put at $3. If the stock declines from 60 to 55 and the investor exercises the put, the profit or loss realized would be _____?

Initially, we can use the Max Chart to recognize the strategy - The investor purchased a put. Now we need to think it through. The stock went down and the investor has the right to sell (at the strike price of 60). He would buy the stock in the open market at 55, sell the stock at 60, and we must take into consideration that the put had a cost of $3.

	Money In	Money out	
Stock	+ 6,000	- 5,500	
Option		- 300	
	------------	------------	
	+ 6,000	- 5,800	= + $200

Stock Split Effects on Options Positions

When a stock splits or a stock dividend is paid, options contracts must be adjusted to reflect this. Either the number of contracts or the shares underlying the contracts will be affected.

For an even split, the number of contracts that the investor owns will increase and the strike price will decrease. Example: An investor owns 1 March 40 call. After a 2-for-1 split, he will own 2 March 20 calls.

For an odd split, the number of shares represented will increase while the exercise price decreases. Example: An investor owns 1 March 30 call. After a 3-for-2 split, he will own 1 March 20 call representing 150 shares.

For a reverse split, the strike price will increase, the shares represented decreasing. Example: An investor owns 1 March 10 call. After a 1-for-5 split, he would own 1 March 50 call representing 20 shares.

Most people seem to grasp an even split. Increase the contracts and decrease the strike price. A memory device that can be applied to the odd and reverse stock splits is to think, "Apply the fraction to the shares, then apply the reciprocal to the strike price". Or simply "Shares, then strike price".

That is, with an odd split, start at the shares with the actual fraction (3-for-2 in a 3-for-2 odd split), apply it, and then move left applying the reciprocal to the strike price.

For a reverse split, you would use the same process. Start at the shares with the actual fraction (1-for-5 in a 1-for-5 reverse split), apply it, then move left applying the reciprocal to the strike price.

Even:

    1 March 40 call   becomes:
    2 March 20 calls

Odd:

    1 March 30 call for 100 shares   becomes:
              2/3 ⟵ 3/2
    1 March 20 call for 150 shares

Reverse:

    1 March 10 call for 100 shares   becomes:
              5/1 ⟵ 1/5
    1 March 50 call for 20 shares

A good memory device for an adjustment for stock dividends would be to again start from the right moving left and thinking "times" and "divide". For example, if a company distributed a 25% stock dividend:

Stock Dividend:

    1 March 30 call for 100 shares   becomes:
          /1.25 ⬅— x 1.25
    1 March 24 call for 125 shares

To summarize this section (memory device):

EVEN = Contracts increase, strike price decreases

ODD = Apply to the shares, reciprocal to strike price

REVERSE = Apply to the shares, reciprocal to strike price

DIVIDEND = Apply to the shares, opposite to strike price

Options Paperwork and Timing:

A question that may appear on your exam has to do with account opening and the paperwork involved in options trading:

-Advertisements must be submitted to the self-regulatory organization 10 days prior to use.

-A Risk Disclosure Document (Characteristics and Risks of Standardized Options) must be given to the customer at or prior to the time that the account is approved.

- An Options Account Agreement (verifies customer's financial information) must be signed by the customer and returned within a 15 day period.

You can think of this as "10 @ 15", or simply apply common sense when using this:

Advertisements will come before sales. Look for the wording "prior to use". The customer must be informed of the risks, therefore, the risk disclosure document would be "at or before" the time that the account is approved. Lastly, the customer has to agree to abide by the rules of the Options Clearing Corporation, and "must be returned within a 15 day period".

Imagine a customer sitting at your desk opening an options account, you can imagine that he saw an advertisement ten days earlier. You want to inform the customer of the risks, so you slide the risk disclosure document across your desk. This is "At or prior" to the account approval. The customer now has "15 days" in which to return his agreement, or he will not be allowed to open another options position.

Applying Your Skills

The key to passing the Series 7 is practice exams. If a candidate is scoring in the 60's taking the practice exams, there's a very good chance that they will score in the 60's on the actual exam. If they are scoring in the 90's, there's a very good chance that they will score in the 90's on the actual exam.

I stated earlier that before you can figure out the answer to the question, you have to understand **what position the investor even has in the first place.** The added benefit of working with the two-step process of recognizing the position, then applying it to the chart, **forces** you to recognize what it is that you are working with. This alone is half the battle.

At this point, I would like to ask you to pull out a blank piece of white paper. Write out the chart. Then take your sponsor-supplied practice exams and **take only the options questions**, checking each answer as you complete each question.

Conclusion

A brief search of the internet reveals that the pass rate for the Series 7 examination is roughly 65%.

This means that 35% of the candidates study the material presented to them, only to fail.

In this book and in the accompanying audio file I have attempted to address what I see as the number one obstacle to obtaining a stockbroker's license. It is my sincere hope that this book combined with your sponsor's study material will help you pass your test and achieve your license.

I would like to thank you for reading this book, and I wish you every success.

Mark

RESOURCES

Options Industry Council (optionseducation.org)

The Options Industry Council is an industry cooperative which provides education to investors, financial advisors and institutional managers on the on the use of exchange-listed equity options. The organization offers options seminars, videos, podcasts, website, and educational literature, as well as live help from options professionals.

Chicago Board Options Exchange (cboe.com)

CBOE is the first and largest options exchange, and the leader in options education. The organization offers quotes and data, tools, education, and trading resources.

Options Clearing Corporation (optionsclearing.com)

The Options Clearing Corporation is the world's largest equity derivatives clearing organization. The organization clears transactions for exchange-listed options, security futures and OTC options. In addition to clearing services, the organization offers education and market data.

Financial Industry Regulatory Authority (finra.org)

FINRA is the largest independent securities regulator in the U.S. The association offers information on the tests that it administers, education, arbitration and mediation. The association is dedicated to investor protection, education, and maintaining fair and honest markets.

Securities and Exchange Commission (sec.gov)

The Securities and Exchange Commission is the primary overseer and regulator of the U.S. securities markets. The organization offers a wealth of educational information for investors.

Made in United States
Orlando, FL
26 July 2024

49569169R00035